Help with HOMEWORK

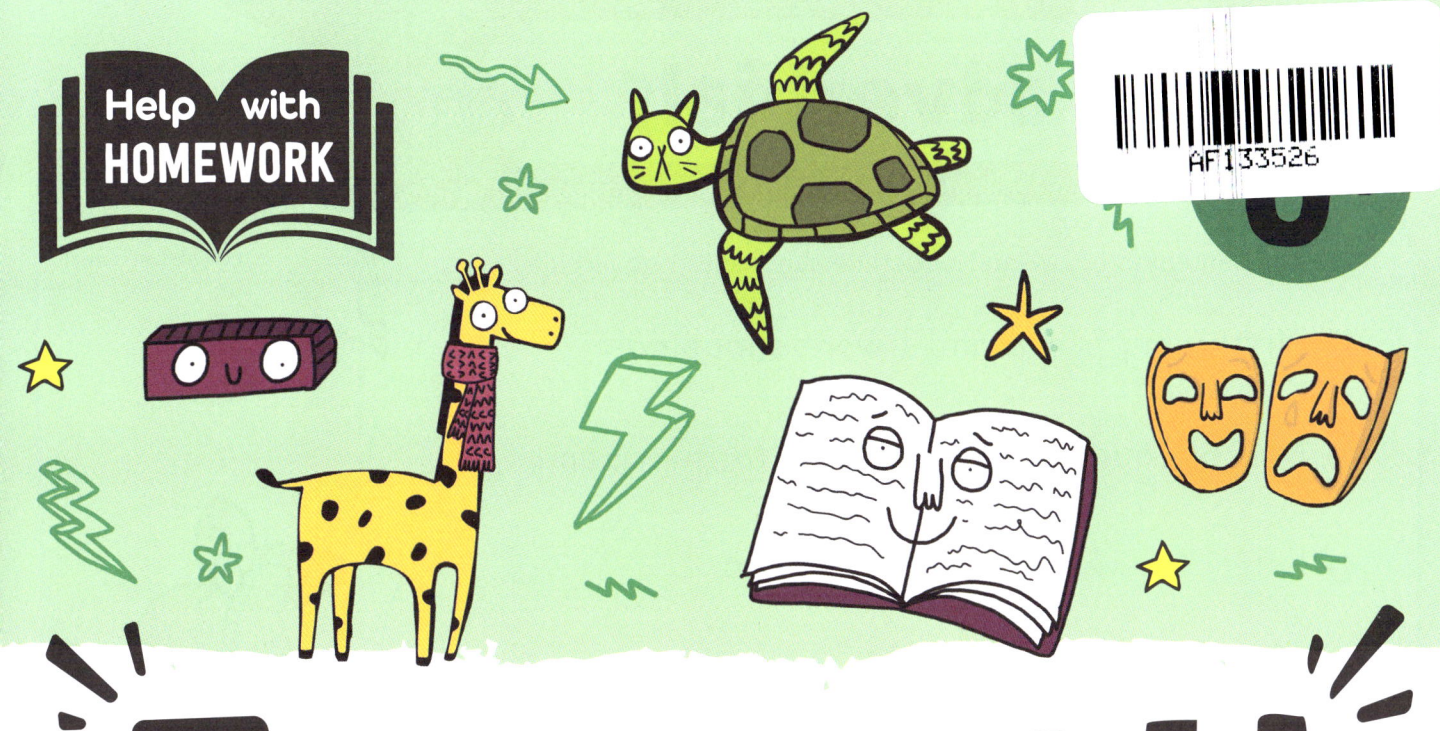

ENGLISH

Practise essential Key Stage 2 English skills

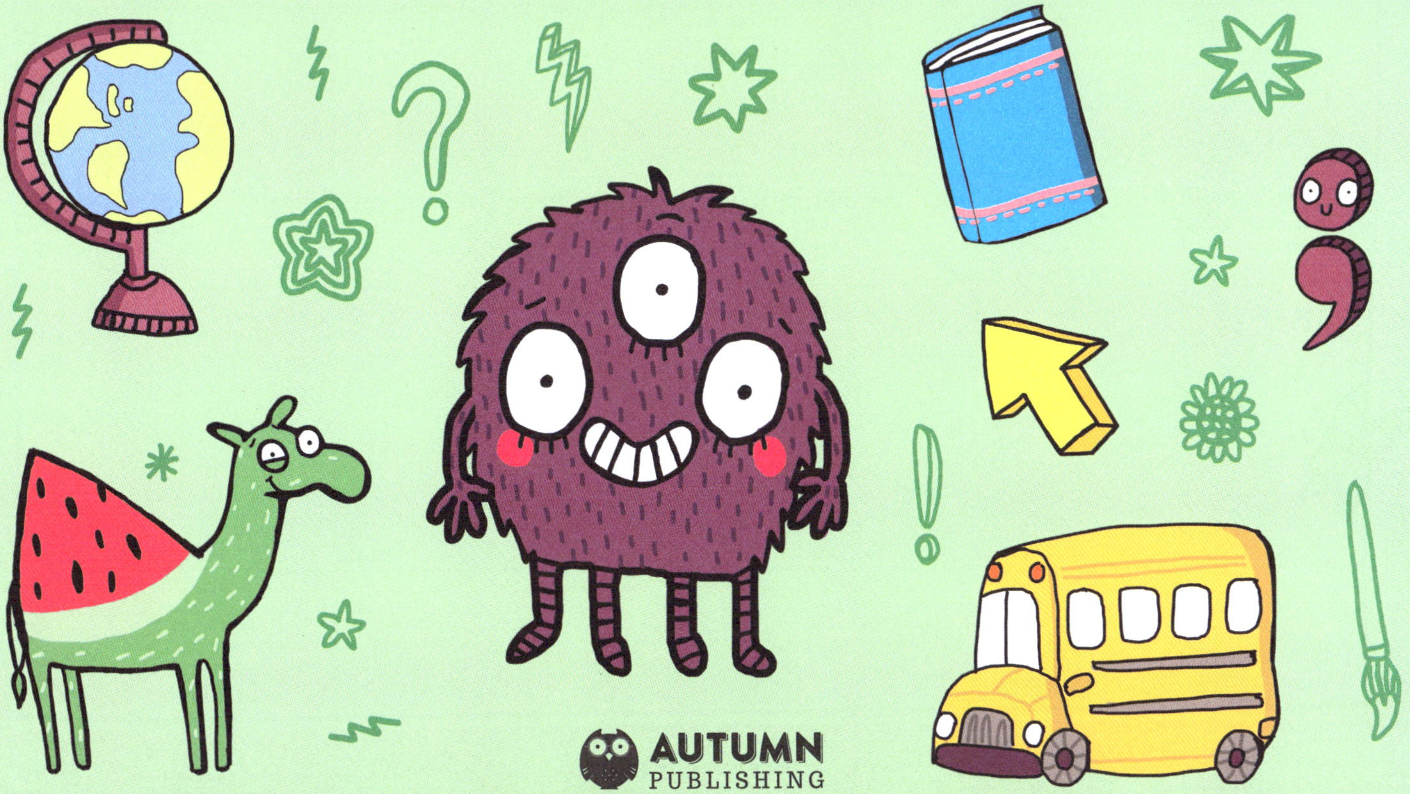

AUTUMN PUBLISHING

Fronted adverbials

When you've finished, give yourself a reward sticker!

Read the sentences below and underline the fronted adverbials.

1. Firstly, my friend and I went shopping.

2. Nearby, our parents went out to the cinema.

3. Later, we went to the cinema too.

4. Excitedly, we ate so much popcorn!

5. Finally, it was time to go home.

6. At home, we watched another film.

Categorise the fronted adverbials from questions 1–6 into when, where or how.

When: ....

Where: ....

How: ....

Write a paragraph about your weekend, using at least three fronted adverbials.

....
....
....
....
....

STICK A REWARD STICKER HERE

2   Answers on page 31

Relative clauses

Relative clauses can be added to a sentence to give more detail about a noun. Relative clauses begin with a relative pronoun (who, when, where, which, that, whose). When a relative clause is in the middle of a sentence, commas are sometimes used around the clause.

For example:
Grandad, **who loved baking**, had made a tasty chocolate sponge cake.
The school, **which was very old**, was the largest in the county.

Relative clauses can come at the end of a sentence, too. When they are at the end of a sentence, a comma generally isn't used.

For example:
I love the food **that my mum cooks.**

Add relative clauses to the sentences below. Remember to add commas.

The teachers .... **marked books all lunchtime.**

The friends .... **went to the local park.**

The staircase ....
.... **was very tiring to walk up and down!**

The pig ....
was very pleased with himself.

The mountain ....
looked picturesque.

Silent letter search

When you've finished, give yourself a reward sticker!

Find the following silent letter words in the grid below:

| column | knock | foreign | sign | doubt |
| guess | half | talk | wrong | honest |

o	a	j	g	e	f	c	d	k	s	f	z
c	o	l	u	m	n	b	h	n	i	a	f
f	o	r	e	i	g	n	k	o	g	h	i
g	c	d	s	e	b	h	d	c	n	d	a
j	g	i	s	h	t	a	l	k	c	i	k
l	k	j	h	e	a	l	b	a	o	f	p
w	a	k	w	o	s	f	g	t	n	p	f
r	b	d	s	w	n	e	b	x	m	a	v
a	r	k	n	m	r	e	j	g	c	q	x
v	h	j	n	w	b	o	s	a	f	b	t
d	o	u	b	t	c	d	n	t	m	j	q
g	h	a	d	q	m	b	c	g	t	x	y

What is the only kind of dog you can eat? A sausage dog!

STICK A REWARD STICKER HERE

Words with 'ough'

This is the trickiest letter string as it makes so many different sounds (or/ow/oo/uff/oh). Read these words, then draw a line to the sound that the **ough** letter string makes. The first one has been done for you.

1. though
2. through
3. although
4. brought
5. enough
6. plough

- or
- oo
- uff
- oh
- ow

The dog has chewed up all the **ough** words! When he spat them back out, they were all jumbled up. Can you put the letters back in the correct order?

7. gohtuh ....
8. ouhgtb ....
9. oudgh ....
10. ghtuhto ....
11. ougnht ....
12. rghou ....
13. ougneh ....
14. uchog ....

What kind of dog likes taking a bath? A shampoodle!

Answers on page 31

To, too or two?

Look at the sentences below and circle the correct words in each one.

1. I would love **to / too / two** go **to / too / two** the Moon.

2. We had to walk in a line, **to / too / two** by **to / too / two**.

3. There were three aliens and **to / too / two** monsters.

4. My sister went **to / too / two** the theme park and I wanted **to / too / two** go **to / too / two**.

5. When the spaceship stopped, we quickly got off but forgot our **to / too / two** suitcases!

6. My parents went **to / too / two** the space museum, and my cousin and I went **to / too / two**.

Place the rocket sticker from the sticker sheet in the space below. Write three of your own sentences about the rocket using the words **to**, **too** and **two**.

When you've finished, give yourself a reward sticker!

Answers on page 31

Possibility

Modal verbs can be used to indicate degrees of possibility. Add the modal verb stickers from the sticker sheet to the appropriate sentences below.

1. It _____ rain in the next ten years.

2. It _____ snow tomorrow.

3. It _____ be sunny in the next week.

4. I _____ drive a car this week.

5. I _____ eat chocolate within the next two days.

6. I _____ play with my friends tomorrow.

7. I _____ read a book this week.

8. The weather _____ be warm tomorrow.

9. My cat _____ eat a dinosaur.

10. My dog _____ play with his toys.

Answers on page 31

Super Spellings

When you've finished, give yourself a reward sticker!

Look at each word, then cover it with your hand and re-write it.

deceive	solemn	
conceive	accompany	twelfth
receive	amateur	variety
perceive	nuisance	ancient
ceiling	occupy	controversy
plough	privilege	correspond
doubt	queue	

More Super Spellings

Here are some more words for you to practise.

curiosity	existence	competition
definite	foreign	protein
determined	harass	seize
develop	identity	vegetable
embarrass	rhyme	stomach
environment	soldier	bargain
excellent	caffeine	autumn

Commas

When you've finished, give yourself a reward sticker!

Place comma stickers in the correct places in these sentences to clarify the meaning. The first one has been done for you.

1. The girl stands up, waves and calls to her friends.

2. The bear reads learns and enjoys improving his knowledge.

3. The unicorn eats chews and spits out apples.

4. The chameleon eats moves slowly changes colour walks and sleeps.

Place a robot sticker from the sticker sheet in the space, then write five sentences about the robot. Use adjectives and commas in the correct places.

Semi-colons

A semi-colon is used instead of a full stop between two sentences to link them together. The sentences below are missing semi-colons. Place a semi-colon sticker in the correct place in each sentence.

1. We kept scoring own goals we lost the football match.

2. She ate three plates of chocolate cake she felt sick afterwards.

3. I'll be there as soon as I've finished my homework that's a promise.

4. He has finished making the main course now he has to make dessert.

Place a robot sticker from the sticker sheet in the space, then write three of your own sentences about the robot. Use a semi-colon in each sentence.

Answers on page 31

11

Plurals

Change the words below into their plural forms, then write the plurals into the correct column of the table.

1. animal ....
2. elf ....
3. shelf ....
4. loaf ....
5. calf ....
6. echo ....
7. human ....
8. spider ....
9. shoe ....
10. half ....

−s	−es	−ves

Finish the descriptions of the pictures below using the correct plurals. The first one has been done for you.

 11. two sheep

 13. three ....

 12. two ....

 14. lots of ....

STICK A REWARD STICKER HERE

Answers on page 31

Hyphens

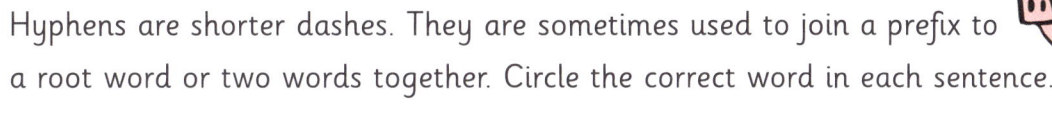

Hyphens are shorter dashes. They are sometimes used to join a prefix to a root word or two words together. Circle the correct word in each sentence.

1. She **re-covered / recovered** the chair with new fabric.

2. It took me ten weeks to **re-cover / recover**.

3. I bought a snack from the **hot dog / hot-dog** seller.

4. The shark eats humans. It's a **man eating / man-eating** shark.

Add a hyphen in the correct place in each sentence below.

5. The children cooperated.

6. The submarine reemerged.

7. The alien reentered the ship.

8. She reedited her essay.

9. The teacher coordinated the lessons.

Write a sentence using a word with a hyphen.

....

....

What do you call a sleeping cow?
A bull dozer!

Parenthesis

Use dashes, commas or brackets to indicate parenthesis in the sentences below.

❶ After eating dinner   but before bedtime   Josh watched television.

❷ Once they'd brushed their teeth   for exactly two minutes   they got their pyjamas on.

❸ The cat   who was good at running   escaped from the dog.

❹ Earth   which is home to more than 7 billion humans   is in a solar system with seven other planets.

Write a sentence using dashes to indicate parenthesis.

....

....

Write a sentence using commas to indicate parenthesis.

....

....

Write a sentence using brackets to indicate parenthesis.

....

....

Whose or who's?

Whose or **who's** are tricksters because the apostrophe here **doesn't** indicate possession. Use thumbs-up stickers to show which one should go in the sentences below.

1. They looked at the boy **whose / who's** shoes were muddy.

2. **Who's / Whose** coming to the ice cream van?

3. **Whose / Who's** coat is this?

4. The girl ran over to the shopkeeper, **whose / who's** dog jumped up at her.

5. My dad, **who's / whose** great at baking, had flour all over his apron.

6. Have you got time to help this student **who's / whose** dropped all her books?

7. This is my friend, Lucy, **who's / whose** going to Spain on holiday.

Fact or opinion?

Place the lion sticker from the sticker sheet in the space below. Read each sentence below and decide whether it is a fact or opinion. Label each one with the correct sticker from the sticker sheet.

1. Lions look scary.

2. A group of lions is called a 'pride'.

3. Lions eat meat.

4. I like lions.

Place the turtle sticker from the sticker sheet in the space below, then write two facts and one opinion about the turtle.

....

....

....

Write two facts and one opinion about the elephant.

....

....

....

When you've finished, give yourself a reward sticker!

STICK A REWARD STICKER HERE

Page 6

Page 10-11

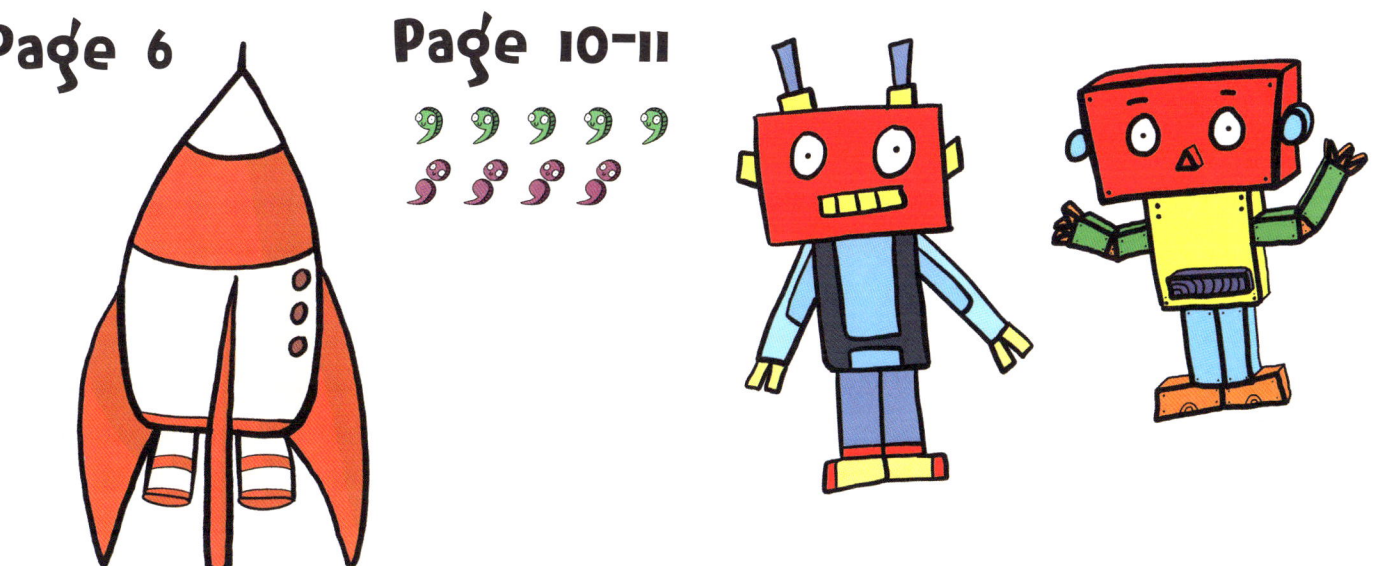

Page 7
will probably   will probably   will probably   will not
could   may   might   might   will   will certainly

Pages 15, 17

Page 16

Page 17

fact   fact   opinion   opinion

Page 18

Page 29 non-fiction young adult fiction children's fiction

Reward stickers

Extras

Being formal

Place a thumbs up sticker next to each formal sentence below.

❶ [ ] I insist that you attend the event this evening.

❷ [ ] You've got to go to the party.

❸ [ ] Can't you make cakes?

❹ [ ] Do you find baking a challenge?

❺ [ ] I must complete my daily exercise regime.

❻ [ ] I'll go for a run soon.

Why can't you play cards in the African Savannah? Because of all the cheetahs!

Place the giraffe sticker from the sticker sheet in the space below, then write one formal sentence and one informal sentence about it.

....

....

....

....

STICK A REWARD STICKER HERE

Answers on page 32

Writing lists

Sam needs to buy some items at the supermarket. He has made a list of them using a colon and semi-colons. Can you find the sticker for each item and place them below for Sam?

At the shop, I need to buy: fizzy pop; a burger; a jar of jam; an onion and a sponge cake.

Can you make a list of the items below using a colon and semi-colons?

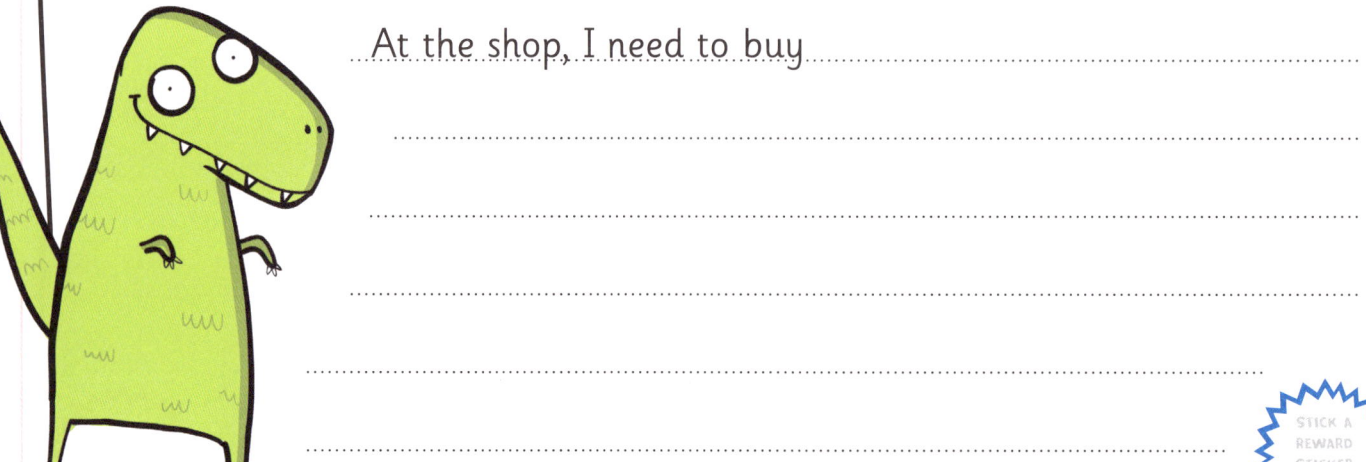

At the shop, I need to buy

Metaphors and similes

The text below uses metaphors and similes. Find and underline them.

The girl was as brave as a lion. She ran through the forest at high-speed like a super-fast racing car. Just as she came to a clearing in the trees, she heard noises. Looking up, she saw a huge dinosaur. It looked scary but it carefully leaned down and shook her hand!

"It's nice to meet you," the girl said.

"It's nice to meet you, too," the dinosaur replied. "Are you hungry?"

"Yes!" said the girl. "I've been in this forest for a long time and I'm feeling blue."

"Here's some food." said the dinosaur, passing the girl some apples. "My stomach's a bottomless pit, but it's good to share."

Now write two metaphors and two similes about these characters.

What do you call a sleeping dinosaur? A dino-snore!

Simile: ....

Metaphor: ....

Simile: ....

Metaphor: ....

Answers on page 32

A recount

When you've finished, give yourself a reward sticker!

Read the following recount.

When I arrived home, I noticed that the garden gate was open. I had definitely locked it the night before. I walked slowly through the open gate, looking carefully. It was very dark so I had to squint to see what was going on. Suddenly, I saw the most surprising sight! There was a fully-grown camel in my garden! I didn't know what to do, but the camel looked very confused, so I walked back out of the garden the way I'd come in, and shut the gate behind me. After that, I called the police.

Now answer the questions about the recount.

1. What adverbials of time have been used in the recount? ....
....

2. What tense (past, present or future) is the text written in? ....

3. Is the text written in first, second or third person? How do you know? ....
....

Write a short recount about your weekend.
....
....
....
....
....

STICK A REWARD STICKER HERE

Answers on page 32

A formal letter

Write a formal letter to complain to a restaurant that made you wait more than an hour for your food. Make it clear why you are writing the letter. For example, do you want a refund or a free meal next time you go?

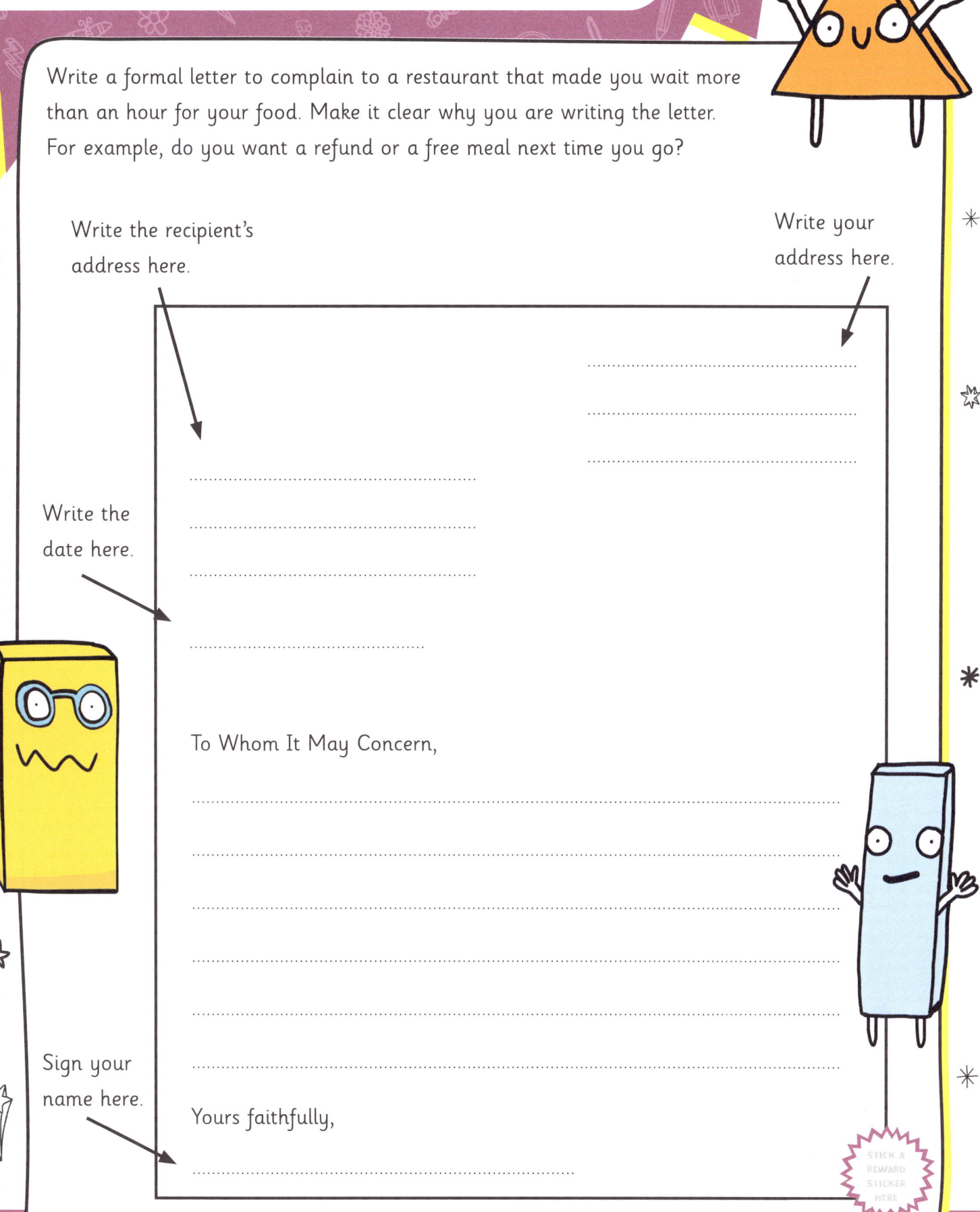

Pet poetry

Draw your favourite pet below.

Write down five adjectives to describe the pet in the boxes below.

Write a short poem about the pet using the adjectives above. Then find a friend or teacher who would like to listen to you perform your poem out loud.

....

....

....

....

....

When you've finished, give yourself a reward sticker!

STICK A REWARD STICKER HERE

Non-fiction

Read the non-fiction text below, then answer the questions about it.

Introduction
Astronauts are people who are trained to travel in spacecraft. Around 500 people have travelled into space so far.

Living in space
Astronauts have to wear special suits so that they can breathe, because there is no oxygen in space. There is also no gravity in space, so astronauts float around. Astronauts have been known to grow up to two inches taller as a result of being in space.

Moon-walking
The following people, among others, have walked on the Moon:
- Buzz Aldrin
- Neil Armstrong
- Pete Conrad

1. How do you know the text is non-fiction?

2. What is the text about?

3. What organisational devices does the text have?

4. What do the organisational devices do?

5. Copy one fact from the text.

Astronaut poster

Now you have read about the topic, create a poster about it. Draw a picture at the top of the poster and include fun facts.

When you've finished, give yourself a reward sticker!

STICK A REWARD STICKER HERE

Planning a Story

Plan a short story inspired by the picture to the right. Think about the setting, character(s), atmosphere and plot. Also consider how you will use dialogue to convey character and advance the action (that's the exciting part).

Setting

Characters

Atmosphere

Plot

Writing a Story

When you've finished, give yourself a reward sticker!

Write your story using your plan. Remember to give it a title.

....

....

....

....

....

....

....

....

....

....

....

....

....

....

....

STICK A REWARD STICKER HERE

Proofreading

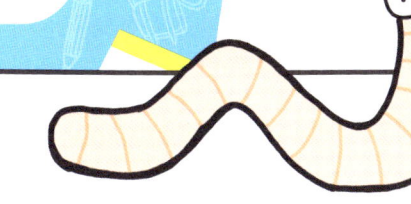

Proofread the text below and correct any spelling or grammar mistakes. Cross through each mistake and re-write it.

the worm finally poked her head up out of the ground.

It had taken her ours, but she had finally found the surface!

She gazed at the forest of soft, green grass and felt so happy

to have escaped the underground tunnels Just as

she started to wigle her way

through the grass to a nearby

bush, the ground started to trembl.

Was it a bird? Was it a human? The worm didn't have time

to find out. She plunged her head back into the soil

and burowed down thruogh the earth, wiggling back

to her home. Oh well, she thort.

Maybe I'll have more luck tomorow.

Answers on page 32

Understanding ideas

When you've finished, give yourself a reward sticker!

Answer the questions below about the last book you read.

1. Who was the main character? How do you know?
   ....
   ....

2. What was the climax of the story?
   ....
   ....

3. How did the story end?
   ....
   ....
   ....

4. How did you think the character felt at the start of the story? What made you think that?
   ....
   ....
   ....

5. How did you think the character felt at the end of the story? What made you think that?
   ....
   ....
   ....

STICK A REWARD STICKER HERE

Comparing books

Below are three different types of book. Label them using the stickers from the sticker sheet, then answer the questions about the books.

❶

❷

❸

❹ Which book is the best for young children? How do you know?

....

....

❺ Which book contains facts?

....

....

❻ Which two books are fictional? How do you know?

....

....

❼ Which book is likely to be the most informal?

....

....

Answers on page 32

What happened next?

When you've finished, give yourself a reward sticker!

Read the text then answer the questions to discuss what you think happens next.

**She pushed open the creaky door. Her sister was behind her, feeling nervous and scared of the dark.
"It's OK!" the big sister said, looking back at her sibling. "Don't be scared."
The sisters walked into the dark hall. As their eyes adjusted to the darkness, they saw a white shape on the far wall.
"A light switch!" the younger sister whispered, running over to it. She reached out her hand and flicked the switch.**

❶ How do you think the younger sister feels at the end of the text?

....

....

❷ What do you think the older sister does next? Why?

....

....

❸ Continue the story in the space below.

STICK A REWARD STICKER HERE

Answers

Page 2: Fronted adverbials
1. Firstly   **2.** Nearby   **3.** Later   **4.** Excitedly   **5.** Finally   **6.** At home
When: firstly / later / finally
Where: nearby / at home
How: excitedly

Page 4: Silent letter search

Page 5: Words with 'ough'
1. though = oh   **2.** through = oo   **3.** although = oh   **4.** brought = or   **5.** enough = uff   **6.** plough = ow
7. though   **8.** bought   **9.** dough   **10.** thought   **11.** nought   **12.** rough
13. enough   **14.** cough

Page 6: To, too or two?
1. I would love to go to the Moon.
2. We had to walk in a line, two by two.
3. There were three aliens and two monsters.
4. My sister went to the theme park and I wanted to go too.
5. When the spaceship stopped, we quickly got off but forgot our two suitcases.
6. My parents went to the space museum, and my cousin and I went too.

Page 7: Possibility
Various possible answers for all questions except for **9.** will not.

Page 10: Commas
2. The bear reads, learns and enjoys improving his knowledge.
3. The unicorn eats, chews and spits out apples.
4. The chameleon eats, moves slowly, changes colour, walks and sleeps.

Page 11: Semi-colons
1. We kept scoring own-goals; we lost the football match.   2. She ate three plates of chocolate cake; she felt sick afterwards.
3. I'll be there as soon as I've finished my homework; that's a promise.   4. He has finished making the main course; now he has to make dessert.

Page 12: Plurals
1. animals   **2.** elves   **3.** shelves   **4.** loaves   **5.** calves   **6.** echoes   **7.** humans   **8.** spiders   **9.** shoes   **10.** halves
11. two sheep   **12.** two rabbits   **13.** three strawberries   **14.** lots of leaves

Answers

Page 13: Hyphens
1. re-covered **2.** recover **3.** hot dog **4.** man-eating **5.** co-operated **6.** re-emerged **7.** re-entered **8.** re-edited **9.** co-ordinated

Page 14: Parenthesis
Various possible answers. For example:
1. After eating dinner – but before bedtime – Josh watched television.
2. Once they'd brushed their teeth (for exactly two minutes) they got their pyjamas on.
3. The cat – who was good at running – escaped from the dog.
4. Earth, which is home to more than 7 billion humans, is in a solar system with seven other planets.

Page 15: Whose or who's?
1. whose **2.** Who's **3.** Whose **4.** whose **5.** who's **6.** who's **7.** who's

Page 16: Fact or opinion?
Fact: A group of lions is called a 'pride'. / Lions eat meat.
Opinion: Lions look scary. / I like lions.

Page 17: Being formal
Sentences 1, 4 and 5 are **formal**. Sentences 2, 3 and 6 are **informal**.

Page 18: Writing lists
At the shop, I need to buy: a bottle of water; two pies; one broccoli; a bottle of tomato sauce; a tin of beans and six cherries.

Page 19: Metaphors and similes
Similes: As brave as a lion / Like a super-fast racing car. **Metaphors:** I'm feeling blue. / My stomach's a bottomless pit.

Page 20: A recount
1. When I arrived home / Suddenly / After that **2.** Past **3.** First person

Page 23: Non-fiction
1. *Your answer could include any of the following:* There are facts; it is written in a formal style; there are sub-headings for each paragraph; there are bullet points.
2. *Your answer could include any of the following:* Astronauts; space; space exploration
3. Sub-headings; bullet points
4. To separate paragraphs into topics or sections; to organise information and facts into easy-to-understand chunks.
5. *Your answer could be any fact from the text. For example:* There is no gravity in space.

Page 27: Proofreading
The worm finally poked her head up out of the ground. It had taken her **h**ours, but she had finally found the surface! She gazed at the forest of soft, green grass and felt so happy to have escaped the underground tunnels. Just as she started to wi**g**gle her way through the grass to a nearby bush, the ground started to tremb**e**. Was it a bird? Was it a human? The worm didn't have time to find out. She plunged her head back into the soil and bur**r**owed down thr**o**ugh the earth, wiggling back to her home. Oh well, she tho**ugh**t. Maybe I'll have more luck tomor**r**ow.

Page 29: Comparing books
1. non-fiction
2. young adult fiction
3. children's fiction
4. Monster Books of Monsters
5. Football: A History
6. *Your answer may be something like this:* Revenge of the Rocktopus and Monster Book of Monsters because they are storybooks and have made up characters.
7. *Your answer may be something like this:* Monster Book of Monsters because it is a children's storybook about funny characters.

Well done!

SKILLS FOR SATS

Practise Key Stage 2 skills in one big workbook

9+

Help with HOMEWORK

AUTUMN PUBLISHING

Adjectives

Adjectives are words that describe the properties of something, such as its colour, size or texture. Choose two different types of adjective to describe each item. Can you use **ing** to turn a verb into an adjective? For example, **buzzing**.

❶ ....

❷ ....

❸ ....

❹ ....

Where do bees catch a bus? A buzz stop!

❺ ....

Read the three sentences below then write some appropriate adjectives to fill in the blanks.

❶ The .... dog chased the .... cat.

❷ The .... girl ate the .... apple.

❸ She wore her .... trousers.

Prefixes

A prefix is a group of letters added to the start of a word to change its meaning. Match the correct prefix stickers to the words below.

1. .... belief
2. .... discovered
3. .... spell
4. .... ravel
5. .... legal
6. .... construct
7. .... behave
8. .... literate

Fill in the table with as many words as you can that contain the prefix at the top of the column. The first one has been done for you.

mis	un	dis
	unexpected	

Answers on page 30

What is it?

When you've finished, give yourself a reward sticker!

Each of these sentences has one word underlined. Label the word as a noun, verb or adjective using the stickers on the sticker sheet. The first one has been done for you.

1. The girl gave her friend a <u>sweet</u>. noun

2. The <u>sweet</u> apple was so delicious!

3. The <u>children</u> read their books quietly.

4. When the <u>children</u> had gone home, the teachers marked their books.

5. The <u>cook</u> made the school dinners every day.

6. I will <u>cook</u> dinner for the family today.

7. Their dog would always <u>bark</u> at trees.

8. She found some <u>tree bark</u> on the floor.

Jelly-fish

Read the two sentences below and label the sections using the stickers on the sticker sheet. Each sentence should have a determiner, noun, verb and adverb.

Camel-on

The	children	read	quietly.

The	dog	barked	loudly.

4   Answers on page 30

Silent letters

Purr-tle

Add silent letters to the spaces to complete the words.

1. wa☐ch
2. ☐our
3. g☐ost
4. ☐rist
5. ☐rote
6. ca☐m
7. g☐ard
8. tong☐e

9. ☐nome
10. ☐night
11. autum☐
12. resi☐n
13. thum☐
14. plum☐er
15. ☐nee

What's a unicorn's favourite snack? Unicorn on the cob!

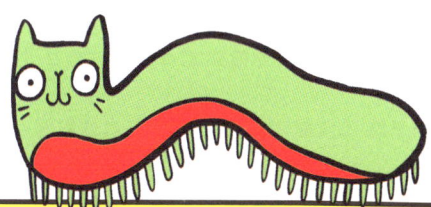
Cat-erpillar

Answers on page 30

Verbs

 Ooooooo!

Verbs are action words. Put a smiley face sticker above the most appropriate verb in each sentence.

1. The boat swam / drove / sailed on the sea.

2. The teachers explained / walked / drank the objective of the lesson.

3. The children ate / played / read the book.

4. Her mum arrived / shouted / hoped at school to pick her up.

Choose appropriate verbs from the box below to fill in the blanks in the text.

| arrived | ran | waved | saw | jumping |

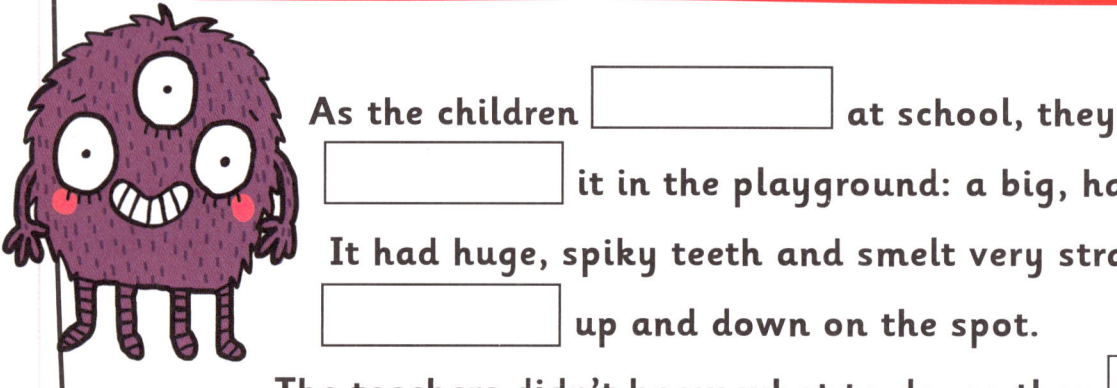

As the children ☐ at school, they immediately ☐ it in the playground: a big, hairy monster! It had huge, spiky teeth and smelt very strange. It was ☐ up and down on the spot.

The teachers didn't know what to do, so they ☐ back into the classrooms and locked the doors. One child walked straight up to the monster and ☐ at him. He looked confused but smiled back.

In the distance, police car sirens could be heard getting nearer and nearer. That's when the monster got scared. It ran.

Answers on page 30

Adverbs

Adverbs tell us more about a verb. They modify it to say when, how or where the action took place. Choose an adverb from the box to fill in the blanks in these sentences. Use each adverb only once.

> angrily   quietly   loudly   softly   quickly

❶ The dog looked .... at the cat then pounced.

❷ The friends spoke .... on the phone so that their parents didn't hear.

❸ The wind blew .... and woke the child up.

❹ The boy tiptoed .... across the hall so that the floorboards didn't creak.

❺ The monster ran .... down the road to get away from the alien.

Now write two of your own sentences using adverbs to tell the reader more about the verbs.

....
....
....
....

Answers on page 30

Missing letters

The words below are missing some letters. Can you fill them in with the stickers from the sticker sheet?

1. fluffy lam☐
2. thistl☐
3. desert ☐sland
4. candle l☐ght
5. caff☐☐ne
6. veg☐table
7. soldi☐r
8. yac☐t
9. ve☐icl☐
10. sho☐lder
11. roundab☐☐t
12. ban☐na
13. pl☐nt
14. shopping a☐sle
15. running rac☐
16. gold trop☐y
17. re☐ding
18. wildl☐fe
19. fores☐
20. ha☐rstyle
21. ☐nomes
22. swimming po☐l

Misspelt words

The words below are spelled incorrectly. Can you rewrite them so that they are correct?

1. protien
2. seeze
3. bargian
4. competishion
5. relevent
6. sacrifise
7. stomack
8. appel
9. cabbege
10. countreyside
11. mountin

How many tickles does it take to make an octopus laugh? Tentacles!

Answers on page 30

Suffixes

A suffix is a group of letters added to the end of a word to change its meaning. Look at these root words and suffixes. Write the new word next to each one.

1. instruct + or = ...
2. act + or = ...
3. sudden + ly = ...

Remember, when the root word ends in **e** and you want to add a suffix that starts with a vowel, you drop the **e**. Add these words and suffixes together. The first one has been done for you.

4. hope + less = **hopeless**
5. move + ment = ...
6. observe + ant = ...
7. observe + ation = ...
8. care + ing = ...

If the root word ends with a single vowel followed by a single consonant, double the consonant when adding a suffix. Complete the words below:

9. sit + ing = ...
10. stop + ed = ...
11. big + est = ...

Suffix patterns

I'm purrr-ple!

Words ending **able** follow a suffix pattern. Fill out the **ly** and **tion** words below. The first one has been done for you.

1. adorable — adorably — adoration
2. applicable — .... — ....
3. considerable — .... — ....
4. tolerable — .... — ....

Fill in the blanks in these sentences using some of the words above.

The kitten was .... and I kept looking at her in ....

It was a .... amount of time before our .... to adopt the kitten was processed.

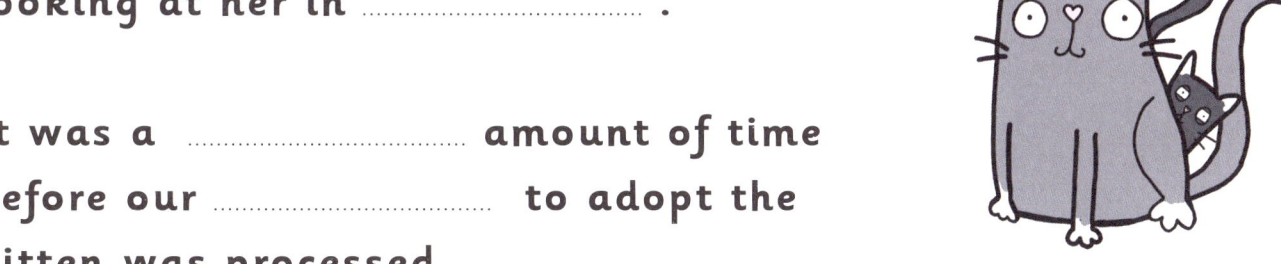

When we could finally take the kitten home, we were nervous that our dog would not be very ...., but he was very gentle.

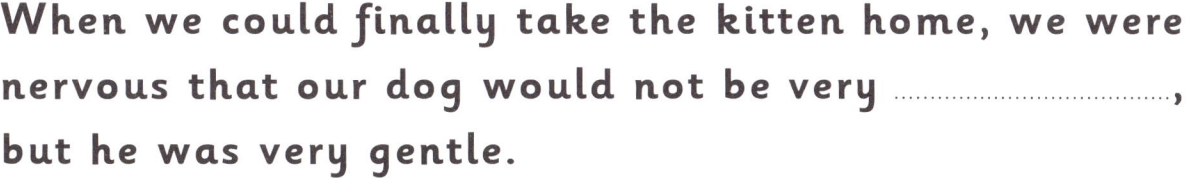

Write your own sentence below using three of the words with suffixes.

....
....

Homophones

Homophones are words that sound the same but mean different things. Put a thumbs-up sticker next to the correct word for each definition below.

When you've finished, give yourself a reward sticker!

1 a current of air

draught ☐   draft ☐

2 out loud

aloud ☐   allowed ☐

3 an island

aisle ☐   isle ☐

4 a gangway between seats

aisle ☐   isle ☐

5 a first attempt at something

draught ☐   draft ☐

6 to change

altar ☐   alter ☐

7 a piece of furniture in a church

altar ☐   alter ☐

8 something permitted

aloud ☐   allowed ☐

Answers on page 30

STICK A REWARD STICKER HERE

Conjunctions

A conjunction is a connecting word (sometimes called a connective) that links clauses or sentences.

For example:
I love running. I hate cycling.
I love running but I hate cycling.

Use a conjunction to combine each pair of sentences into one sentence.

1 The school bus was late. It broke down before we got to school.

....

2 I take the bus to school bus every day. I prefer to cycle.

....

3 My friend goes on the bus. He doesn't have a bike.

....

4 I like to eat my sandwiches on the school bus. I get hungry.

....

5 One of my friends has never taken the bus to school. She walks.

....

6 The bus driver is friendly. He likes his job.

....

Answers on page 30

Expanded noun phrases

Expanded noun phrases tell you more about the noun. Complete the table of expanded noun phrases below. Use strong adjectives and interesting prepositional phrases.

ADJECTIVE	NOUN	PREPOSITIONAL PHRASE
bright	sun	in the morning
	apple	in the fruit bowl
	monster	
shiny	robot	
	unicorn	

Create a MISSING poster for a dog who has escaped. Place the dog sticker from the sticker sheet into the space, then use strong adjectives to describe the dog.

MISSING

Ending in...

The words below either end in **ge** or **dge**. Match each word to the correct ending. The first one has been done for you.

- ba
- do
- bri
- villa
- hu
- a
- he
- fu
- sle

- dge
- ge

The words below either end in **el** or **le**. Match each word to the correct ending. The first one has been done for you.

- cam
- squirr
- app
- tow
- jew
- peop
- tunn

- le
- el

What is a camel's favourite nursery rhyme? Humpty Dumpty!

Ordering

Put the cars in order from the smallest number to the largest number using the stickers on the sticker sheet.

When you've finished, give yourself a reward sticker!

❶　　　　❷　　　　❸　　　　❹

Split these numbers into thousands, hundreds, tens and ones:

	Thousands	Hundreds	Tens	Ones
❺ 3964 =				
❻ 1255 =				
❼ 993 =				
❽ 1050 =				
❾ 1004 =				

Write the numbers from questions 5–9 in order from largest to smallest:

....

Answers on page 31

Page 3 dis de mis mis
il il un un

Page 4 adjective noun noun noun noun noun verb verb determiner noun verb adverb determiner noun verb adverb

Page 6

Page 8 a a a b e e e e e g h
h h i i i i i i o t u u

Page 14

Pages 12, 17, 18, 20, 24

Page 16

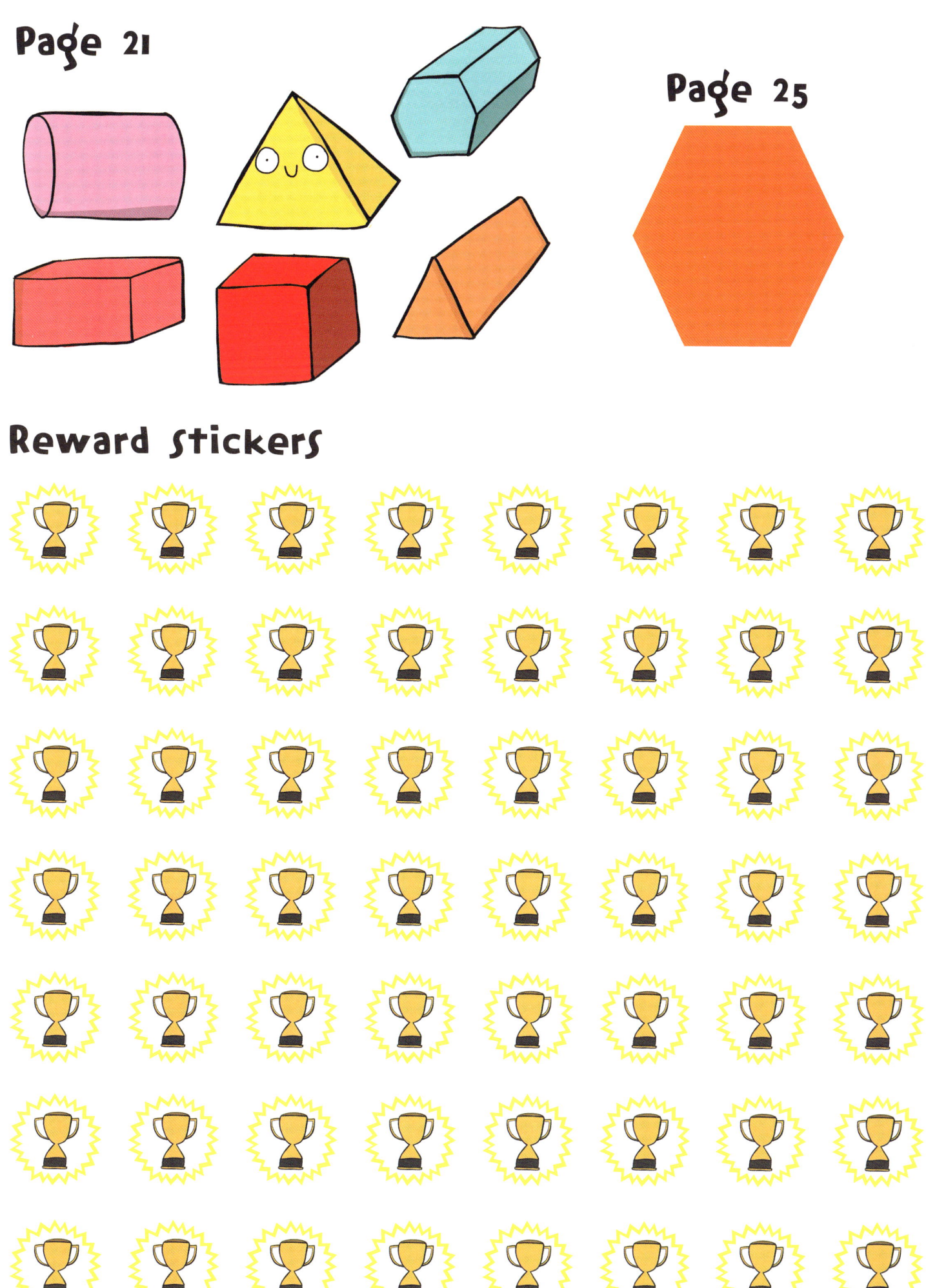

Comparing

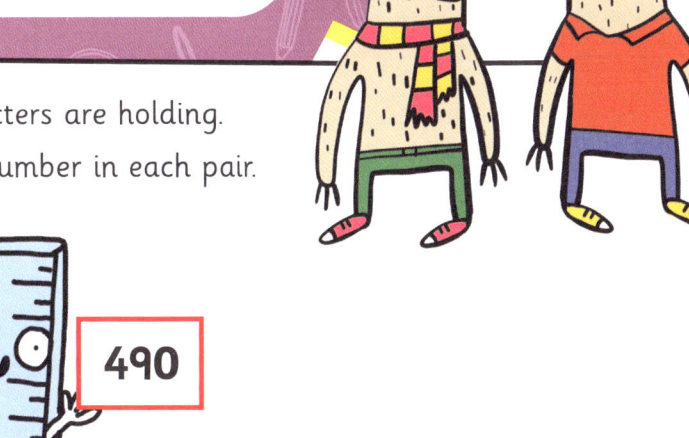

Look at the pairs of numbers that the characters are holding. Put a thumbs-up sticker next to the largest number in each pair.

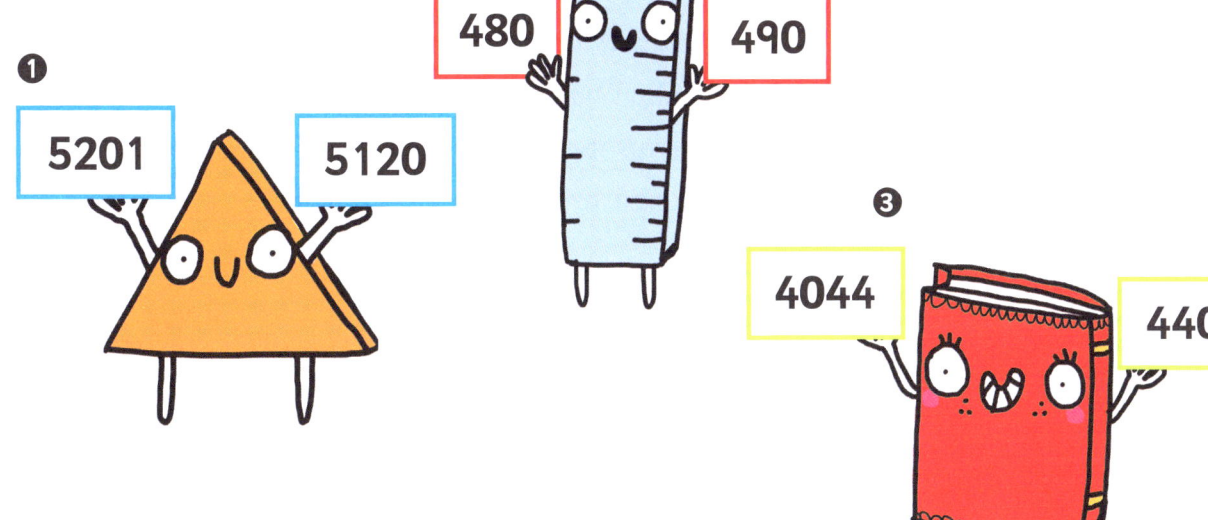

1. 5201 / 5120
2. 480 / 490
3. 4044 / 4404

Look at the pairs of numbers that the characters are holding. Put a thumbs-up sticker next to the smallest number in each pair.

4. 222 / 2222
5. 1920 / 1092
6. 479 / 4979

Prime numbers

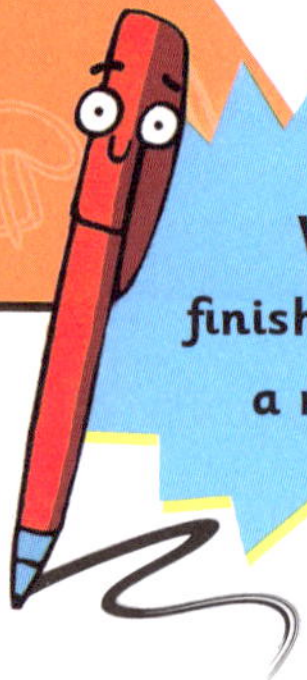

When you've finished, give yourself a reward sticker!

A prime number can only be divided by itself and 1. This alien needs to input all prime numbers up to 19 into his spaceship. Can you help him by completing the list below?

1. 2 .... 3 .... 7 .... 13 .... 19 ....

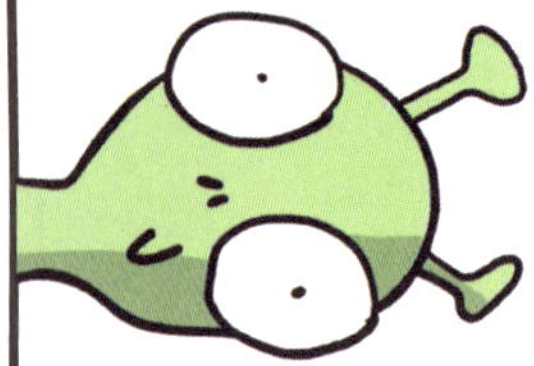

Work out whether these numbers are prime numbers or not. Show your working and explain how you know. When you've worked it out, put a thumbs up sticker next to every prime number and a thumbs down sticker next to the ones that are left.

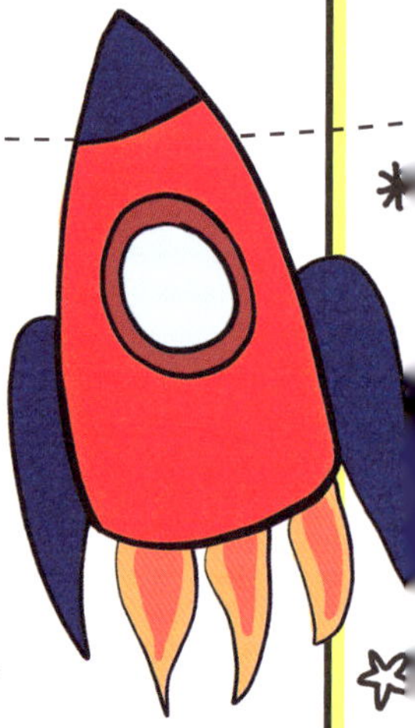

2. 80 ....

3. 79 ....

4. 22 ....

5. 97 ....

6. 98 ....

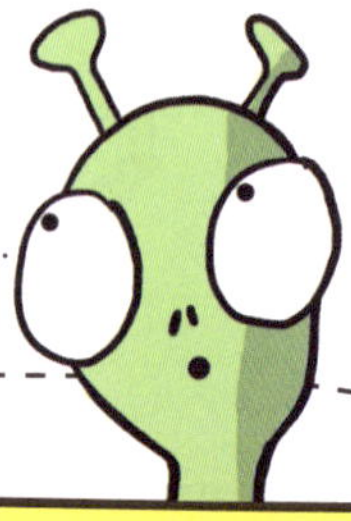

STICK A REWARD STICKER HERE

Answers on page 31

Prime or composite?

A composite number is anything that isn't a prime number. Remember that a prime number can only be divided by itself and one. Look at the numbers below and draw a line to match each one to the correct label. The first one has been done for you.

PRIME NUMBER   COMPOSITE NUMBER

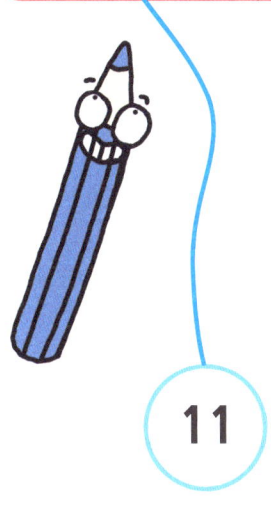

11   70   25   7

40   19   99   72

Write the numbers below as a product of their prime factors. The first one is done for you.

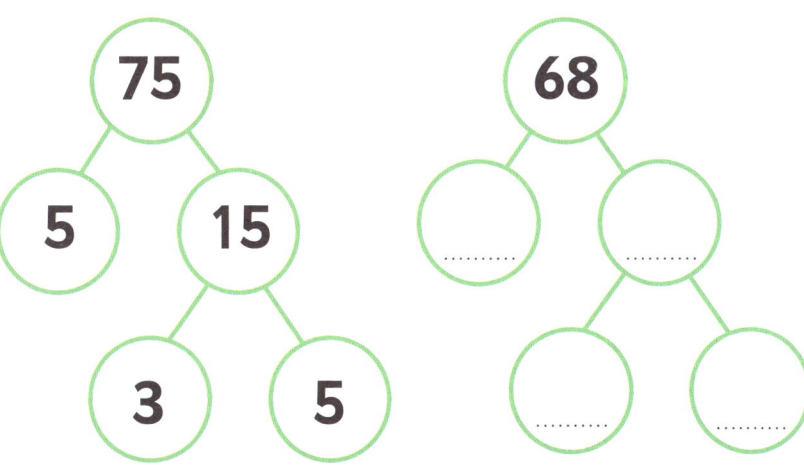

Answers on page 31

2D Shapes

Draw the correct 2D shape under each name.

Triangle

Pentagon

Hexagon

Square

Circle

Octagon

True or false? Give each statement a thumbs-up sticker if it is true, or turn the sticker round and give it a thumbs down if it is false.

❶ Hexagons have six sides.

❷ Squares have four equal sides.

❸ Octagons have nine sides.

❹ Pentagons have the same number of sides as squares.

❺ Circles have one vertex.

Answers on page 31

3D Shapes

Place the correct 3D shape sticker under each name, then write a property of each shape underneath.

Cube

Cuboid

Cylinder

Triangular prism

Square-based pyramid

Hexagonal prism

Answers on page 31

School timetable

The timetable below shows the times of Year 5 lessons for the week. Answer the questions about the timetable below.

	Lesson 1	Lesson 2	B R E A K T I M E	Lesson 3	Lesson 4	L U N C H T I M E	Lesson 5	Lesson 6
Monday	Maths	English		History	Assembly		Geography	Music
Tuesday	English	Maths		Drama	Assembly		History	P.E.
Wednesday	Maths	English		French	Assembly		Music	Art
Thursday	English	Maths		Maths	P.E.		French	R.E.
Friday	English	English		Maths	Assembly		Art	Art

❶ Which days have a History lesson? ....

❷ How many Maths classes are there per week? ....

❸ What are the two most common classes? ....

❹ Is Geography after break time or lunch time? ....

❺ What is straight after English on a Tuesday? ....

❻ How many lessons are there on Wednesdays? ....

❼ Which day has two art lessons? ....

❽ Which day doesn't have assembly? ....

Answers on page 31

Your own table

Make your own timetable for your weekend. Include at least 5 events each day.
For example, events could include reading a book, playing a board game or baking.

	7 am–9 am	9 am–11 am	11 am–1 pm	1 pm–3 pm	3 pm–5 pm	5 pm–7 pm	7 pm–9 pm
Saturday							
Sunday							

Which event do you do most on a Saturday? ....

How many events have you included in total? ....

Are there any time slots where you don't have an event? ....

Draw your own table in the box below to show what you eat throughout a typical day.
You could use the following headings: Breakfast / Snack / Lunch / Tea / Dinner / Dessert.

Reflections

Reflection is a type of transformation where a shape is reflected by a mirror line.

Look at the reflections below. Three are correct and three are incorrect. Place a thumbs-up sticker next to the correct reflections.

When you've finished, give yourself a reward sticker!

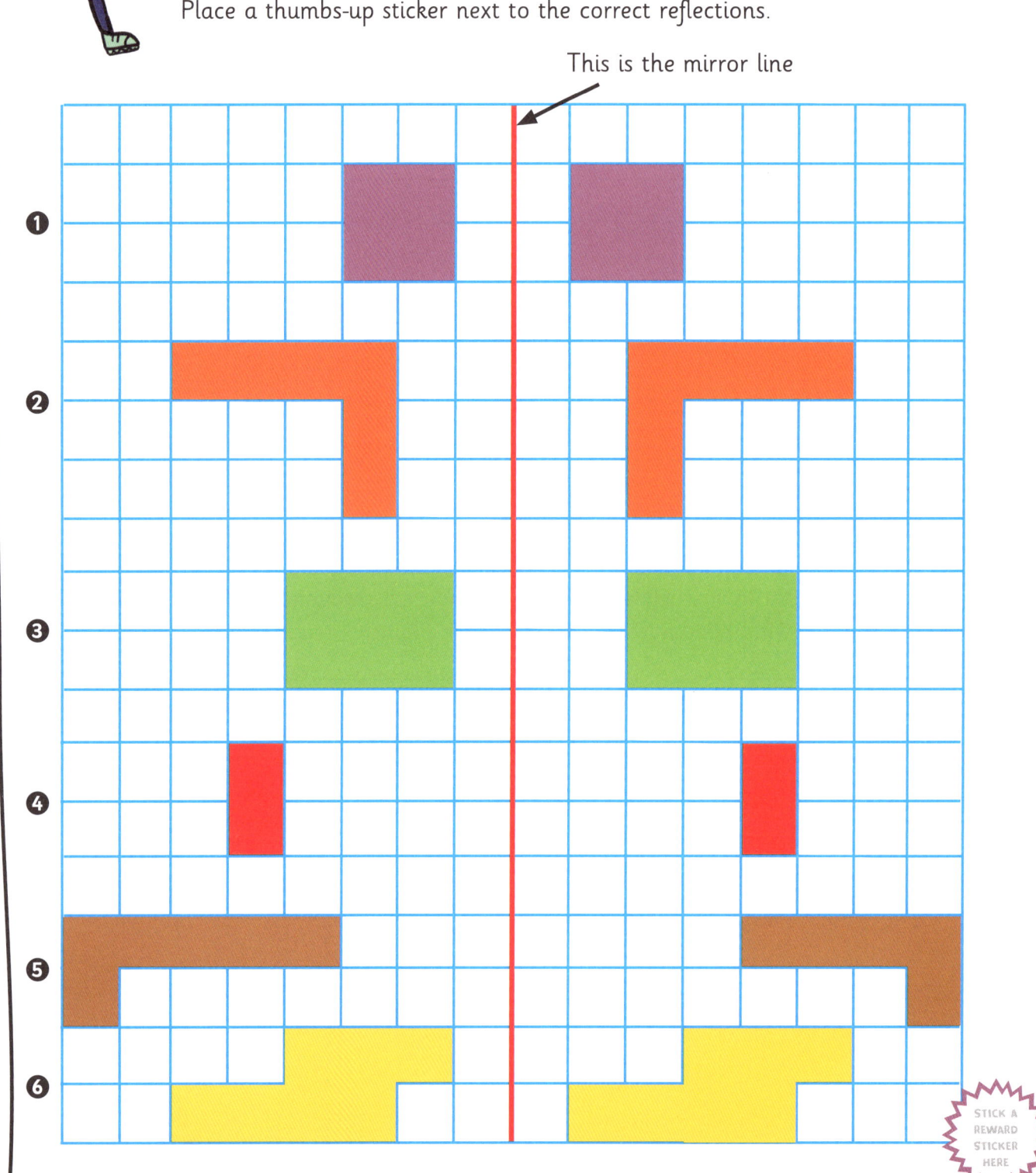

This is the mirror line

Answers on page 32

More reflections

Use the hexagon sticker on the sticker sheet to show the reflection of this shape.

Draw your own shape on the left-hand side then draw its reflection to the right of the mirror line.

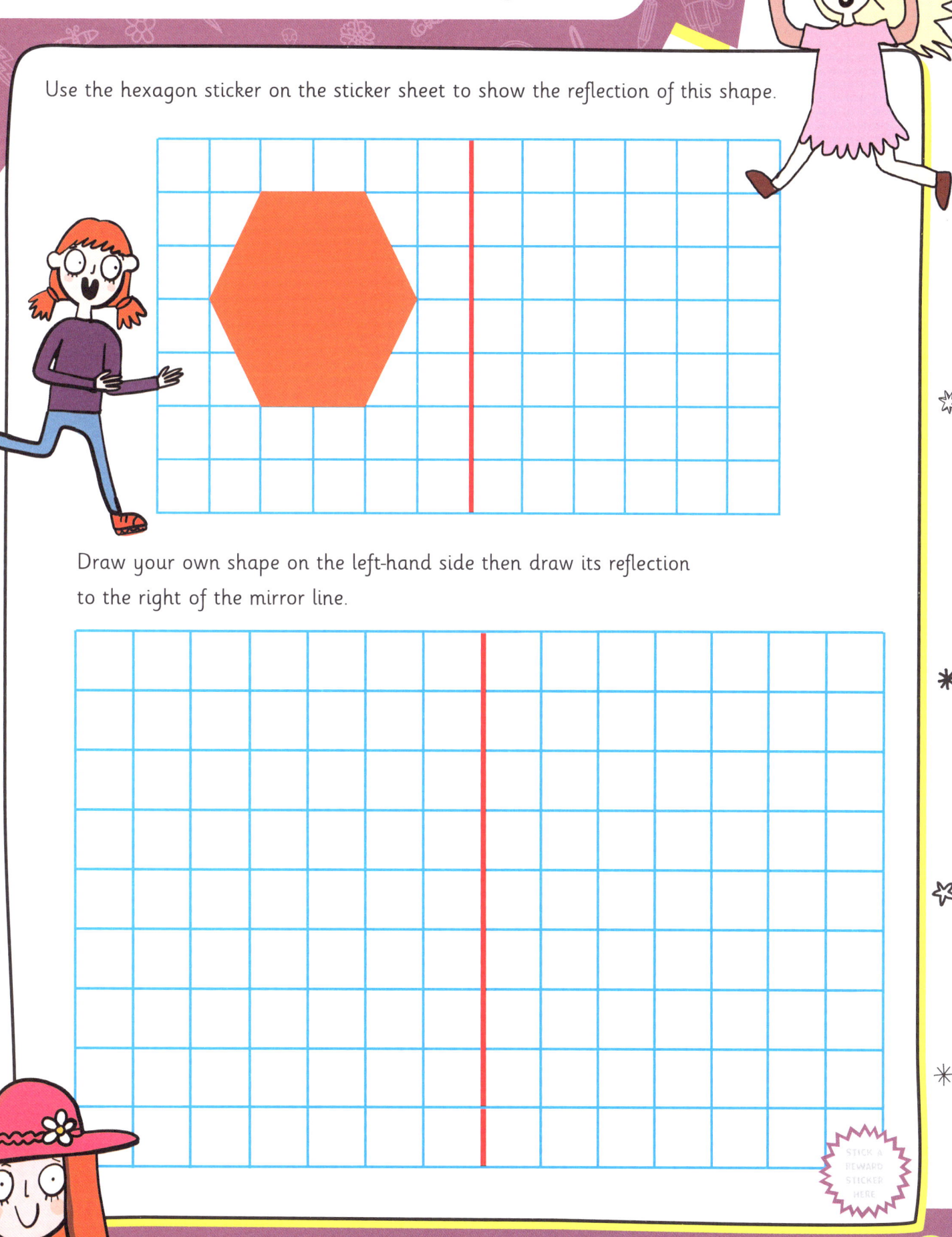

Answers on page 32

Is it mm, cm or m?

When you've finished, give yourself a reward sticker!

Convert the measurements between metres (m) and centimetres (cm).

❶ 6 m = ... cm

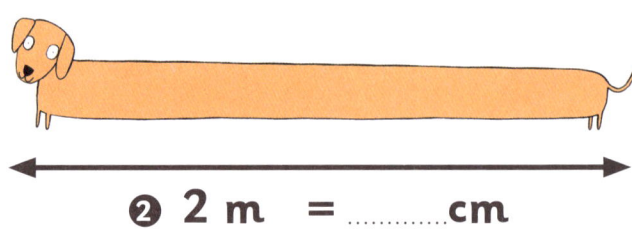

❷ 2 m = ... cm

❸ 50 cm = ... m

Wanda Worm and her friends are trying to work out who is the longest. Can you convert the centimetre (cm) measurements to millimetres (mm)?

❹ Wanda 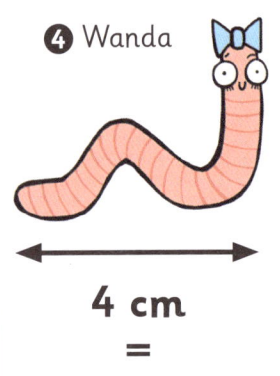 4 cm = ... mm

❺ Wayne  2.5 cm = ... mm

❻ Wyclef 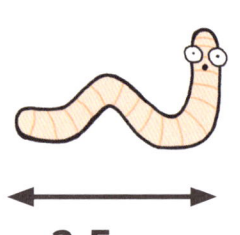 3 cm = ... mm

❼ Willie 3.5 cm = ... mm

❽ Wendy 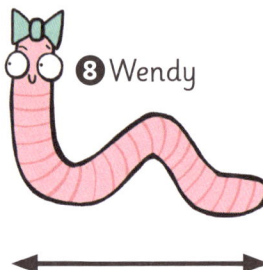 4.5 cm = ... mm

Who is the longest worm? ....

How many millimetres is the shortest worm? ....

Answers on page 32

Jam, grams and kilograms

Convert the jam weight from kilograms (kg) to grams (g), then try the following questions.

We're jammin'!

❸ Each jar holds 2 kg of jam. Clown has made 6000 g of jam. How many jars can he fill? Show your working.

....

....

❶ 2 kg = ... g

❹ If Clown has three jars half-filled with jam and two full jars of jam, how much do they weigh in kilograms?

❷ 1 kg = ... g

....

❺ Clown sells his jars of jam to his friends. One of his friends wants 5 kg of jam. How many jars should Clown give him? Show your working.

....

....

❻ Clown gives his family 6000 g of jam. How much is that in kilograms? Show your working.

....

....

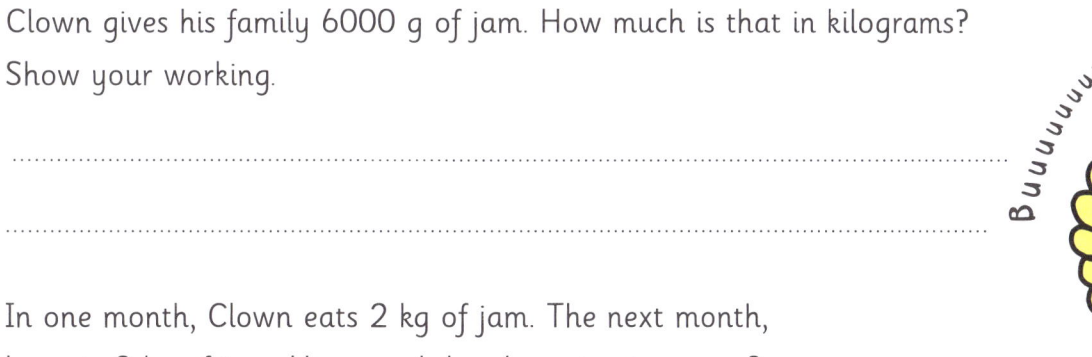

Buuuuuuuuuuurrrrp!

❼ In one month, Clown eats 2 kg of jam. The next month, he eats 3 kg of jam. How much has he eaten in grams?

....

❽ Clown makes a new batch of jam and fills up 120 jars. How many kilograms is that?

....

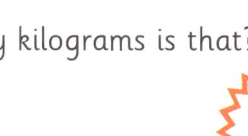

Answers on page 32

Bar charts

When you've finished, give yourself a reward sticker!

A large group of people were asked what their favourite theme park ride is. This bar chart shows the results:

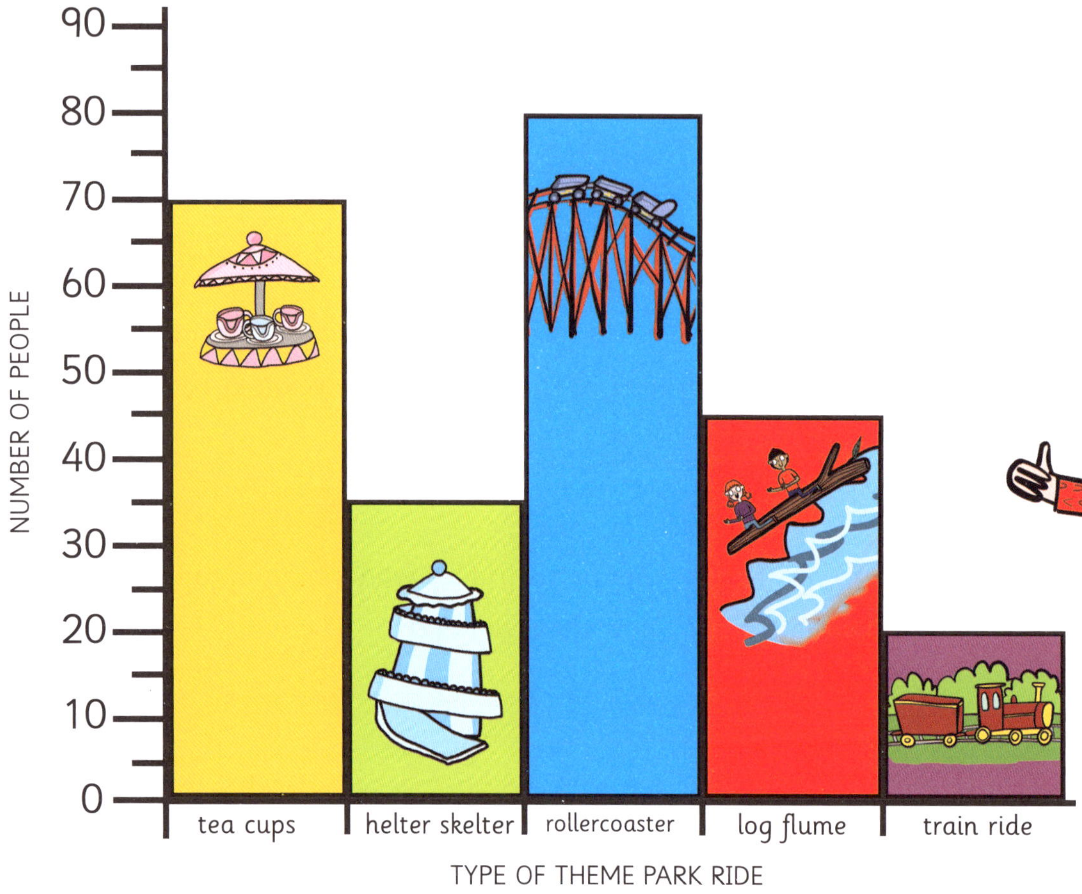

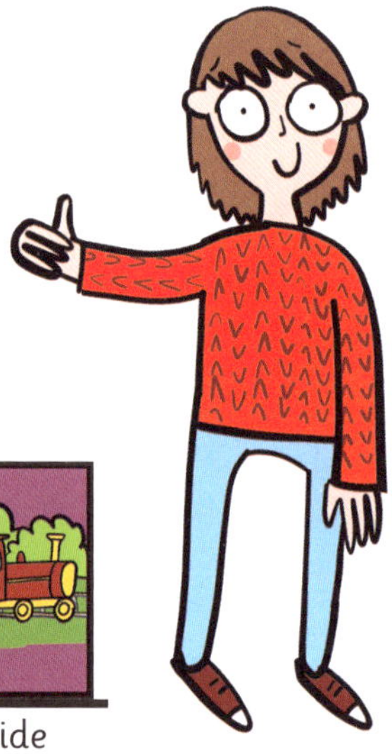

❶ What is the most popular ride? ....

❷ What is the least popular ride? ....

❸ How many people chose the train ride as their favourite? ....

❹ How many people chose the helter skelter as their favourite? ....

❺ Which ride did 45 people choose as their favourite? ....

❻ How many rides are there altogether? ....

STICK A REWARD STICKER HERE

Answers on page 32

Line graphs

This line graph shows the temperature outside Penguin's home.

What do you call a happy penguin? A Pen-grin!

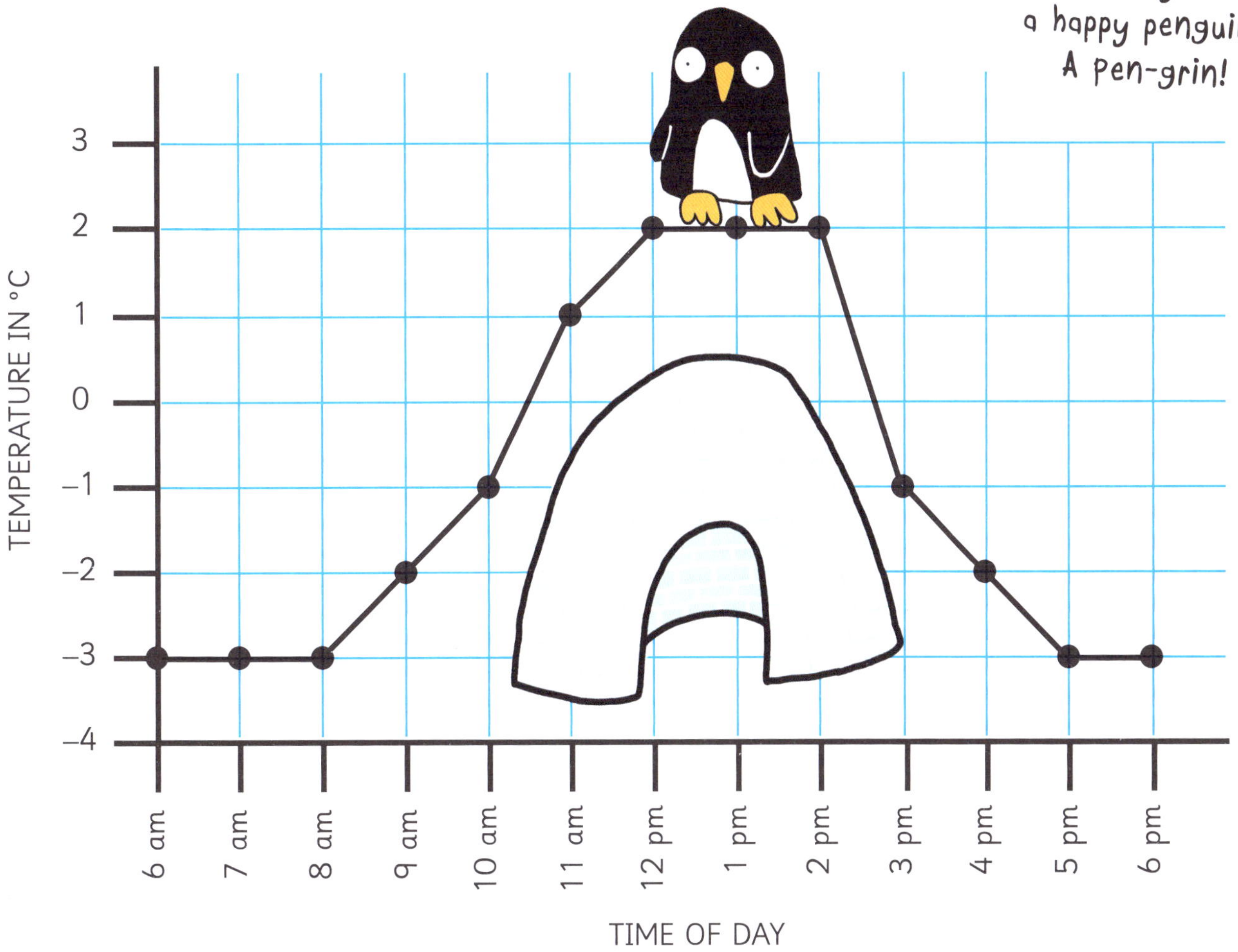

① What temperature was it when Penguin woke up at 7 am? ....

② How many degrees did the temperature increase by between 9 am and 11 am? ....

③ What was the most common temperature between 6 am and 6 pm? ....

④ How many degrees colder was it at 5 pm than 2 pm? ....

⑤ The temperature at 7 pm was 2 degrees colder than at 4 pm. What was the temperature at 7 pm? ....

Answers on page 32

Answers

Page 2: Adjectives
(various possible answers)
1. sour, yellow lemon   2. pink, wiggling worm   3. slow, green tortoise   4. bright, warm sun
5. fuzzy, buzzing bee

Page 3: Prefixes
1. disbelief   2. undiscovered   3. misspell   4. unravel   5. illegal   6. deconstruct
7. misbehave   8. illiterate

Page 4: What is it?
1. noun   2. adjective   3. noun   4. noun   5. noun   6. verb   7. verb   8. noun
The (determiner) children (noun) read (verb) quietly (adverb).
The (determiner) dog (noun) barked (verb) loudly (adverb).

Page 5: Silent letters
1. watch   2. hour   3. ghost   4. wrist   5. wrote   6. calm   7. guard   8. tongue   9. gnome   10. knight
11. autumn   12. resign   13. thumb   14. plumber   15. knee

Page 6: Verbs
1. sailed   2. explained   3. read   4. arrived
arrived / saw / jumping / ran / waved

Page 7: Adverbs
1. angrily   2. quietly   3. loudly   4. softly   5. quickly

Page 8: Missing letters
1. fluffy lamb   2. thistle   3. desert island   4. candle light   5. caffeine   6. vegetable   7. soldier   8. yacht
9. vehicle   10. shoulder   11. roundabout   12. banana   13. plant   14. shopping aisle   15. running race
16. gold trophy   17. reading   18. wildlife   19. forest   20. hairstyle   21. gnomes   22. swimming pool

Page 9: Misspelt words
1. protein   2. seize   3. bargain   4. competition   5. relevant   6. sacrifice   7. stomach   8. apple   9. cabbage
10. countryside   11. mountain

Page 10: Suffixes
1. instructor   2. actor   3. suddenly   4. hopeless   5. movement   6. observant   7. observation
8. caring   9. sitting   10. stopped   11. biggest

Page 11: Suffix patterns
1. adorable > adorably > adoration
2. applicable > applicably > application
3. considerable > considerably > consideration
4. tolerable > tolerably > toleration

The kitten was <u>adorable</u> and I kept looking at her in <u>adoration</u>. It was a <u>considerable</u> amount of time before our <u>application</u> to adopt the kitten was processed. When we could finally take the kitten home, we were nervous that our dog would not be very <u>tolerant</u>, but he was very gentle.

Page 12: Homophones
1. draught   2. aloud   3. isle   4. aisle   5. draft   6. alter   7. altar   8. allowed

Page 13: Conjunctions
Various possible answers. For example: 1. The school bus was late <u>because</u> it broke down before we got to school.

Answers

Page 15: Ending in...
badge / dodge / bridge / village / huge / age / hedge / fudge / sledge
camel / squirrel / apple / towel / jewel / people / tunnel

Page 16: Ordering
The correct order of the race cars is: 2064 (blue), 3064 (green), 3694 (pink), 3964 (red).

5. 3964 =	3000	900	60	4
6. 1255 =	1000	200	50	5
7. 993 =	0	900	90	3
8. 1050 =	1000	0	50	0
9. 1004 =	1000	0	0	4

Correct order: 993, 1004, 1050, 1255, 3964

Page 17: Comparing
1. 5201 **2.** 490 **3.** 4404 **4.** 222 **5.** 1092 **6.** 479

Page 18: Prime numbers
1. 2, 3, 5, 7, 11, 13, 17, 19. **2.** 80: divisible by many numbers so isn't a prime number. **3.** 79: only divisible by 1 and itself so is a prime number.
4. 22: divisible by many numbers so isn't a prime number. **5.** 97: only divisible by 1 and itself so is a prime number.
6. 98: divisible by many numbers so isn't a prime number.

Page 19: Prime or composite?
Prime numbers: 11, 7, 19   Composite numbers: 70, 25, 40, 99, 72

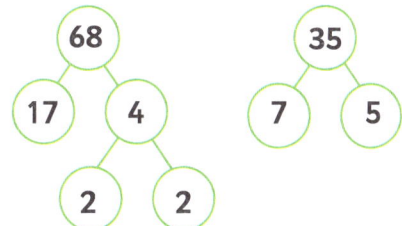

Page 20: 2D shapes

Triangle   Pentagon   Hexagon   Square   Circle   Octagon

True: 1, 2   **False:** 3, 4, 5

Page 21: 3D shapes

Cube   Cuboid   Cylinder   Triangular prism   Square-based pyramid   Hexagonal prism

Cubes have six square faces.   Cuboids have four rectangular faces and two square ones.   Cylinders have two circular ends that are connected by a single face.   Triangular prisms have two triangular ends and are connected by three rectangular sides.   Square-based pyramids have a square base and four triangular sides.   Hexagonal prisms have two hexagonal ends and are connected by six rectangular sides.

Page 22: School timetable
1. Monday and Tuesday **2.** 6 **3.** Maths and English **4.** Lunch time **5.** Maths **6.** 5 **7.** Friday **8.** Thursday

Answers

Page 24: Reflections

1. Correct **2.** Correct **3.** Incorrect **4.** Correct **5.** Incorrect **6.** Incorrect

Page 25: More reflections

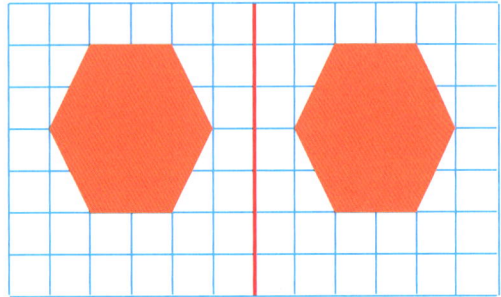

Page 26: Is it mm, cm or m?

1. 600 cm **2.** 200 cm **3.** 0.5 m **4.** 40 mm **5.** 25 mm **6.** 30 mm **7.** 35 mm **8.** 45 mm

Wendy is the longest worm. The shortest worm is 25 mm (Wayne).

Page 27: Jam, grams and kilograms

1. 3 jars **2.** 3 jars half-filled = 3 kg. 2 full jars = 4 kg. So 3 kg + 4 kg = 7 kg in total. **3.** 2000 g **4.** 1000 g
5. Two full jars and one half-full jar. **6.** 6 kg **7.** 5000 g **8.** 120 x 2 kg = 240 kg

Page 28: Bar charts

1. rollercoaster **2.** train ride **3.** 20 **4.** 35 **5.** log flume **6.** 5

Page 29: Line graphs

1. –3°C **2.** 3 **3.** –3 °C **4.** 5 **5.** –4 °C

Well done!

Help with HOMEWORK

9+

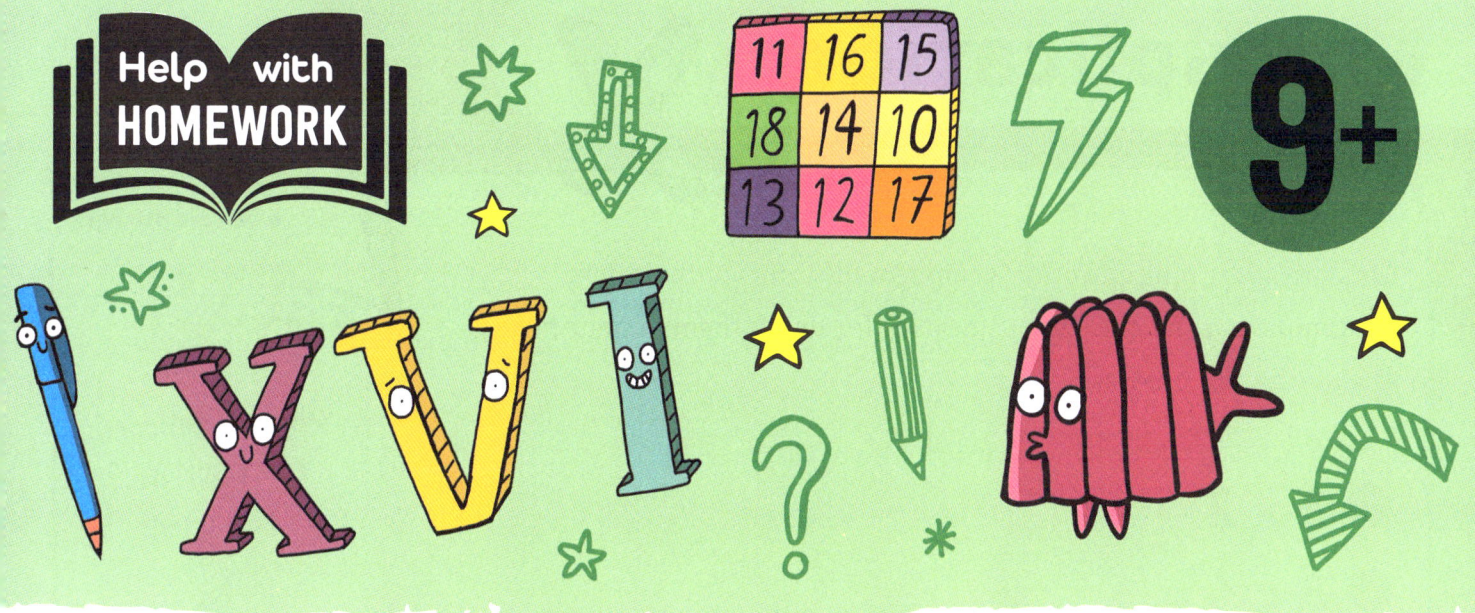

MATHS

Practise essential Key Stage 2 maths skills

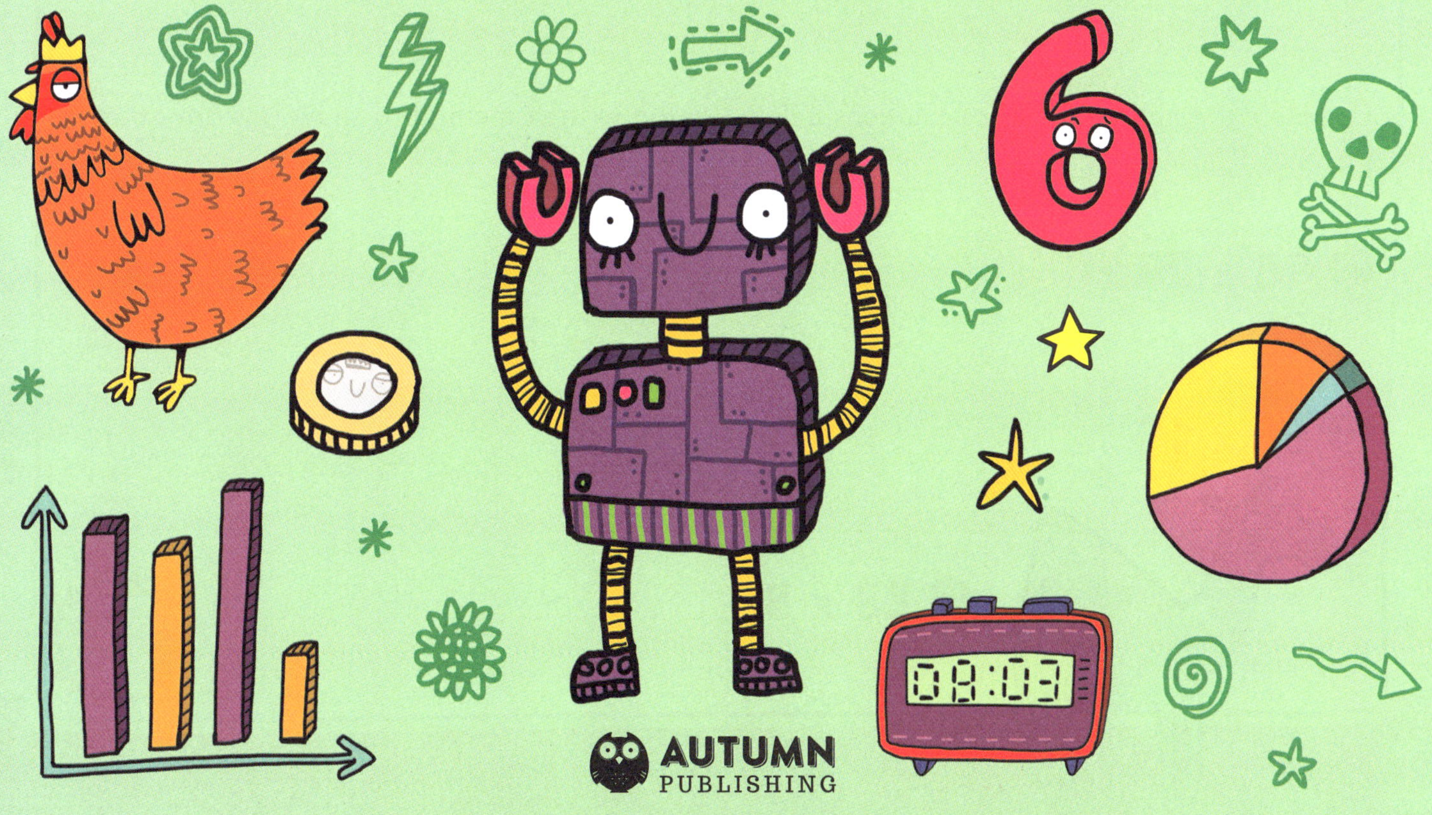

AUTUMN PUBLISHING

Multiplication

When you've finished, give yourself a reward sticker!

Unicorn finds multiplication complicated! Can you help him by completing the calculations below? Try doing them in your head, then write the answers.

What do unicorns call their dad? Pop Corn!

1. 2 x 2 = ...
2. 3 x 4 = ...
3. 5 x 2 = ...
4. 8 x 1 = ...
5. 0 x 6 = ...
6. 8 x 7 = ...
7. 9 x 10 = ...
8. 11 x 4 = ...
9. 6 x 12 = ...

Complete the multiplication calculations below using a written method to show Unicorn exactly how to work them out.

10. 98 x 29

11. 66 x 19

12. 83 x 85

Ca-melon

STICK A REWARD STICKER HERE

Division

Cat-erpillar

Answer the division calculations below.

① 2 ÷ 2 = ...

② 8 ÷ 4 = ...

③ 20 ÷ 2 = ...

④ 8 ÷ 2 = ...

⑤ 6 ÷ 1 = ...

⑥ 24 ÷ 6 = ...

⑦ 42 ÷ 7 = ...

⑧ 12 ÷ 2 = ...

⑨ 56 ÷ 7 = ...

Complete the division calculations below using a written method.

⑩ 100 ÷ 2 ....

Purr-tle

⑪ 117 ÷ 3 ....

⑫ 228 ÷ 4 ....

⑬ 190 ÷ 10

Answers on page 31

Alien addition

These aliens need help with the addition calculations below. Can you fill in the blanks?

1. 120 + ☐40 = 260
2. 175 + 1☐2 = 297
3. 505 + 1☐1 = 606
4. 1000 + 1☐5☐ = 2458

Solve the calculations below:

5. 120 + 40 =
6. 174 + 72 =
7. 805 + 11 =
8. 107 + 105 =

Bleep bloop!

9. 358 + 715 =
10. 573 + 183 =
11. 685 + 18 + 48 =
12. 12 + 485 + 404 =

Answers on page 31

Super Subtraction

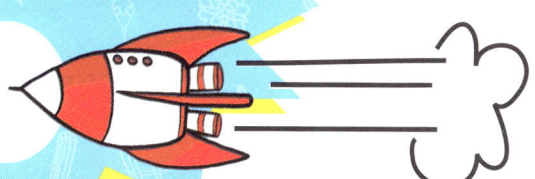

The aliens love eating all sorts of food from Earth. They have filled out the table below which shows how much food they started with and how much they have eaten. Can you work out how much food they have got left?

Food type	Amount started with	Amount eaten	Amount left
Bananas	10	8	
Pizza	3	3	
Apples	48	41	
Ice cream	2	1	
Cherries	49	36	
Burgers	24	20	
Cake	9	8	

On their way back to the spaceship, the aliens find 59 biscuits. One eats 3, the second one eats 9, another eats 19 and the final alien eats 1. How many biscuits are left? Show your working out.

Answers on page 31

Perimeter

Sam wants to put fences around her farm. Can you work out the perimeter of each field? Write each answer in metres and centimetres.

When you've finished, give yourself a reward sticker!

Remember to add all the sides!

1) 9 m, 6 m, 9 m, 6 m
.... m
.... cm

2) 8 m, 7 m
.... m
.... cm

3) 4 m, 8 m
.... m
.... cm

4) 6 m, 5 m
.... m
.... cm

5) 8 m, 9 m
.... m
.... cm

The fence sections Sam will use are 2 m each in length. How many fence sections does she need in total for all 5 fields?

....

Answers on page 31

Area

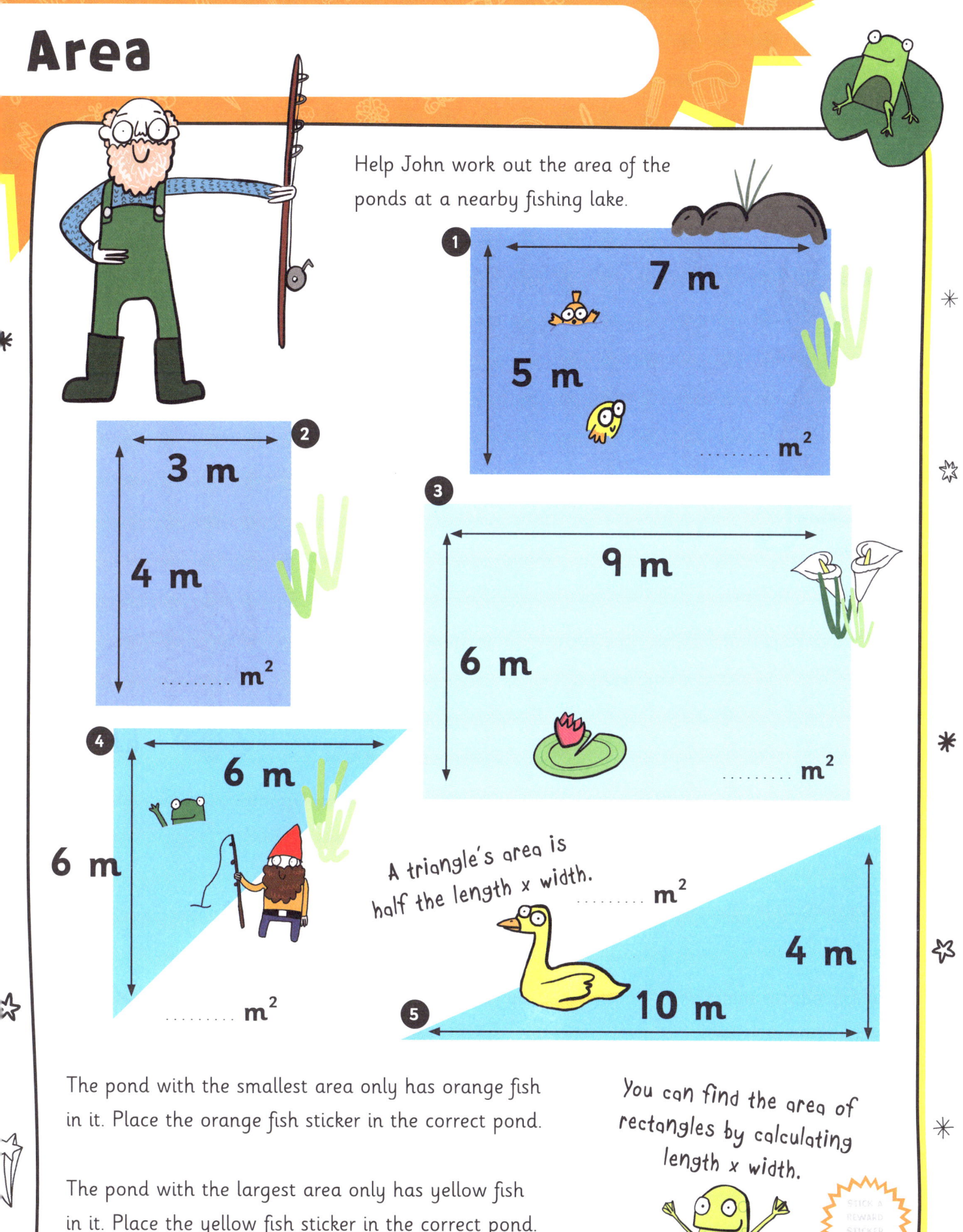

Help John work out the area of the ponds at a nearby fishing lake.

1. 7 m, 5 m, ... m²
2. 3 m, 4 m, ... m²
3. 9 m, 6 m, ... m²
4. 6 m, 6 m, ... m²
5. 10 m, 4 m, ... m²

A triangle's area is half the length x width.

You can find the area of rectangles by calculating length x width.

The pond with the smallest area only has orange fish in it. Place the orange fish sticker in the correct pond.

The pond with the largest area only has yellow fish in it. Place the yellow fish sticker in the correct pond.

Answers on page 31

Square numbers

Work out the square numbers below. The first one has been done for you.

3^2 = 3 x 3 = 9

5^2 = 5 x 5 =

6^2 =

8^2 =

10^2 =

1 T. rex says that 2^2 is 4. Is he correct? Show how you know.

....

....

2 Triceratops has worked out that 11^2 is 22. What has he done wrong? Explain the correct answer.

....

....

3 Diplodocus thinks 7^2 is 49 but T. rex says that 7^2 is 44. Who is correct? Explain how you know.

....

....

....

Cube numbers

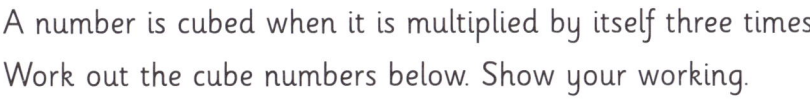

A number is cubed when it is multiplied by itself three times. Work out the cube numbers below. Show your working.

3^3 = 3 x 3 x 3 = 9 x 3 = 27

4^3 = 4 x 4 x 4 = 16 x 4 =

5^3 =

7^3 =

10^3 =

How do you ask a dinosaur to lunch? "Tea, Rex?"

Rawr!

① Diplodocus says that 6^3 is 216. Is she correct? Show how you know.

② T. rex says that 9^3 is 27. What has he done wrong? Explain the correct answer.

③ Triceratops and T. rex try to work out 12^3. Can you show them the best way to work it out and find the answer?

Answers on page 31

Rounding decimals

Round the decimals below to the nearest whole number.

1. 5.39 ....
2. 5.81 ....
3. 2.05 ....
4. 9.92 ....

purrr-ple

Round the decimals below to one decimal place.

5. 4.54 ....

6. 2.11 ....

7. 9.56 ....

8. 8.32 ....

9. 3.92 ....

10. Now put your answers from questions 5–9 in order from lowest to highest.

....

Answers on page 31

Percentages

Answer the multiple choice questions below by placing a thumbs-up sticker next to each correct answer.

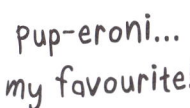
pup-eroni... my favourite!

① $\frac{1}{2}$ as a percentage is   **40%**   **50%**   **60%**

② 30% as a decimal is   **0.3**   **0.5**   **0.03**

③ 0.75 as a percentage is   **55%**   **65%**   **75%**

④ 20% as a decimal is   **0.22**   **0.2**   **0.02**

⑤ If Dog has a whole pizza and she eats half of it, what percentage of the pizza is left?

50%   **90%**   **12%**

⑥ Cat bakes a cake and takes 75% of it to his friend's house. What percentage does he have left at home?

5%   **15%**   **25%**

⑦ Cat-ula makes a pie and cuts it into 10 equal slices. He eats 20% of the slices. What percentage does he have left?

20%   **80%**   **30%**

Vam-purrr

Answers on page 31

Multiplication

When we multiply a number by 10, each digit moves one place value column to the left. When we multiply a number by 100, each digit moves two place value columns to the left.

For example:

1.5 x 10 = 15

1.5 x 100 = 150

100	10	1	.	0.1
		1	.	5
	1	5	.	0

Work out the calculations below.

1. 4.6 x 10 =

2. 4.6 x 100 =

3. 8.8 x 100 =

4. 9.3 x 100 =

5. 8.9 x 100 =

6. 3.75 x 10 =

7. 4.85 x 100 =

8. 9.12 x 10 =

9. 5.55 x 100 =

Division

When we divide a number by 10, each digit moves one place value column to the right. When we divide by 100, each digit moves two place value columns to the right.

For example:

1.5 ÷ 10 = 0.15

1.5 ÷ 100 = 0.015

I need to wear glasses to improve my di-vision.

Help Octopus work out the calculations below.

❶ 460 ÷ 10 = ...

❷ 460 ÷ 100 = ...

❸ 46 ÷ 10 = ...

❹ 930 ÷ 100 = ...

❺ 850 ÷ 100 = ...

❻ 375 ÷ 10 = ...

❼ 485 ÷ 100 = ...

❽ 910 ÷ 10 = ...

❾ 555 ÷ 100 = ...

 Jelly-fish

Answers on page 31

Rounding whole numbers

When you've finished, give yourself a reward sticker!

Round these numbers to the nearest 10.

1. 127 = ...
2. 382 = ...
3. 4992 = ...
4. 1124 = ...

Round these numbers to the nearest 100.

5. 496 = ...
6. 493 = ...
7. 399 = ...
8. 114 = ...

Round these numbers to the nearest 1000.

9. 4995 = ...
10. 3811 = ...
11. 3002 = ...
12. 6039 = ...

Answers on page 31

Roman numerals

Number	1	5	10	50	100	500
Roman numeral	I	V	X	L	C	D

Use the stickers on the sticker sheet to change the numbers below into Roman numerals, then write them out in words. The first one has been done for you.

1. 10 = X = ten
2. 20 = =
3. 50 = =
4. 100 = =
5. 150 = =
6. 200 = =
7. 230 = =
8. 265 = =
9. 380 = =
10. 550 = =

Answers on page 31

Angles in triangles

An angle is a measure of turn, or rotation, around a point. We can measure an angle using a protractor.

There are four types of angles:
- Right angle (a quarter turn)
- Acute angle (less than a quarter turn)
- Obtuse angle (between a quarter and a half turn)
- Reflex angle (more than a half turn)

If you add up the angles in a triangle, you always get 180°.

Use calculations to work out the missing angles in these triangles (not to scale).

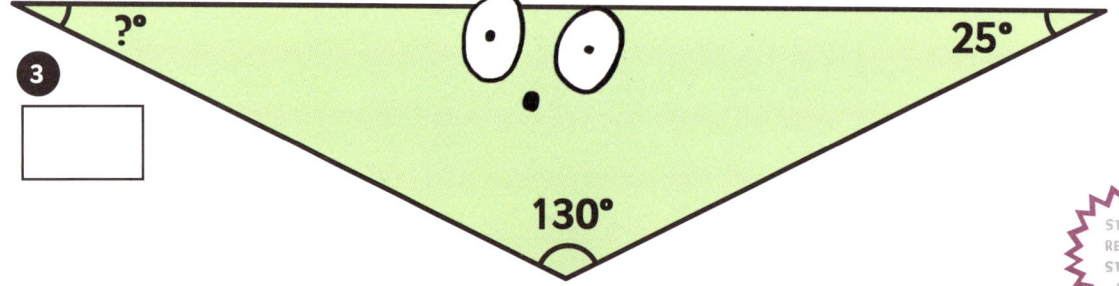

When you've finished, give yourself a reward sticker!

Page 7

Page 11

Page 15

V X X X X X X X X X X X L L L
L L C C C C C C C C C C C D

Page 19

Page 20

regular   regular   regular   regular
irregular   irregular   irregular   irregular

Page 22

Page 24

Pages 24 & 25

1 3 3 6 6 7 7
8 12 12 13 13 17 18
20 21 23 23 25 37

Page 30

Moon A
24.5 km
circumference

Moon B
57.1 km
circumference

Moon C
21.09 km
circumference

Moon D
21.9 km
circumference

Moon E
57.7 km
circumference

Reward Stickers

Missing angles

Can you work out the missing angles below? Remember that angles on a straight line add up to 180° and angles around a point add up to 360°.

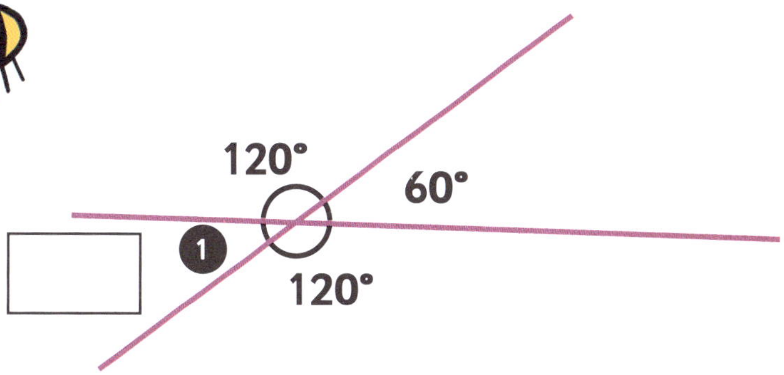

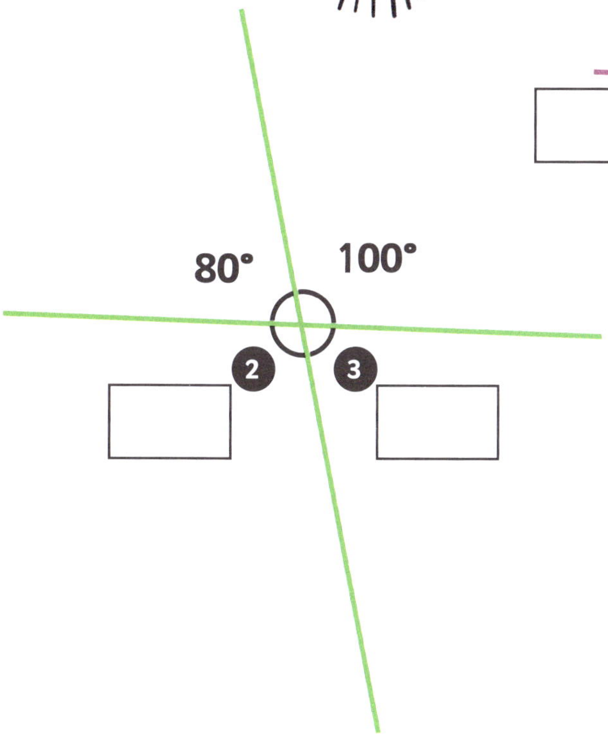

1. 120°, 60°, 120°
2. 80°
3. 100°
4. 100°, 80°
5. 30°, 180°

What's a bear without bees? An ear!

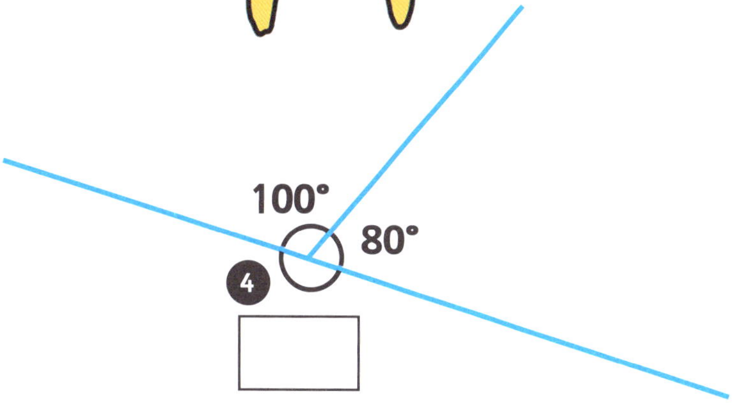

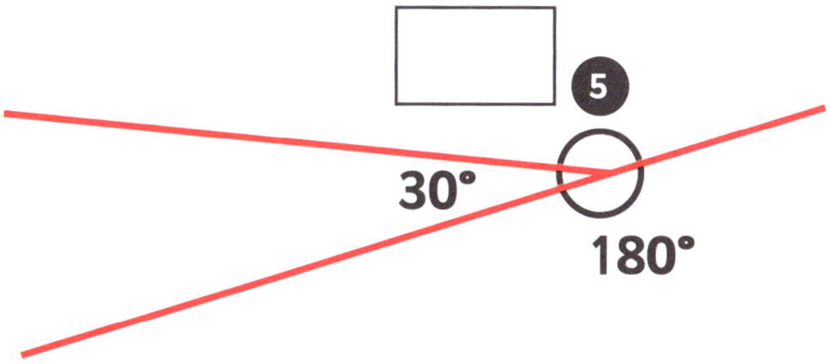

Answers on page 32

17

Reading scales

When you've finished, give yourself a reward sticker!

Can you read the thermometers below? Write the temperature on the dotted line for each one?

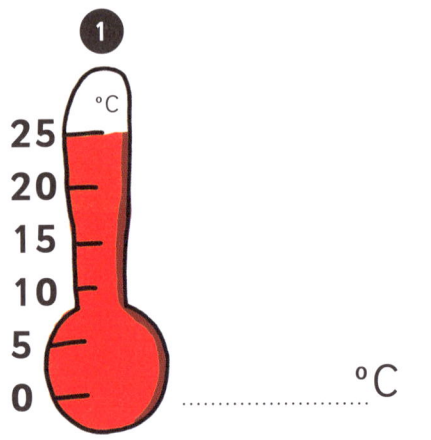
1. .... °C

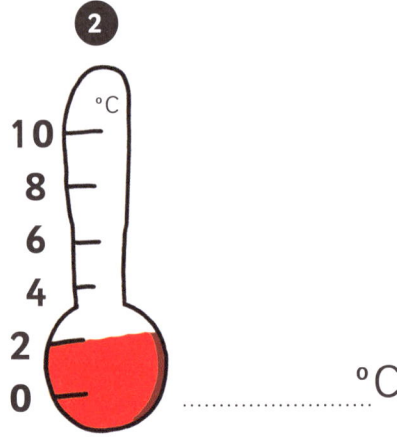
2. .... °C

3. .... °C

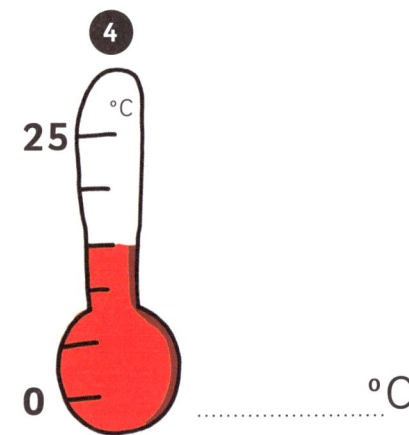
4. .... °C

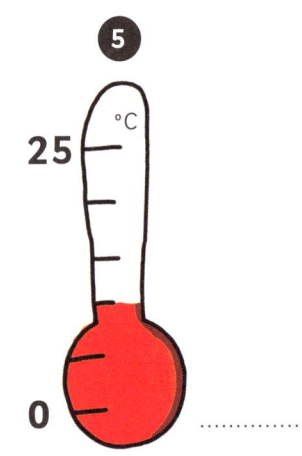
5. .... °C

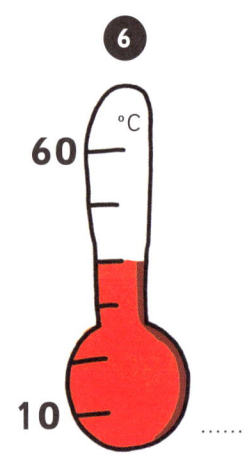
6. .... °C

Answers on page 32

Pirate coordinates

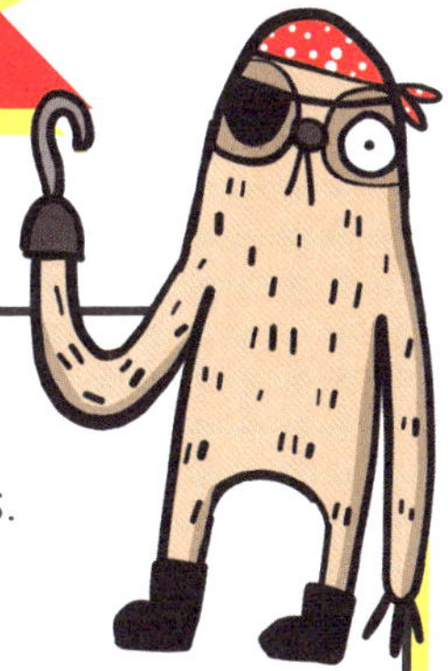

Captain Sloth has forgotten where his treasure chests are buried! Use the coordinates below to work out where you should place the treasure chest stickers. One has been done for you.

(–5,6) (4,4) (–2,–3) (2,2) (–3,–3) (1,1)

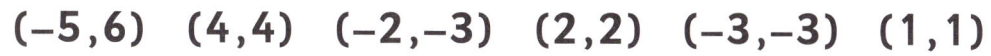

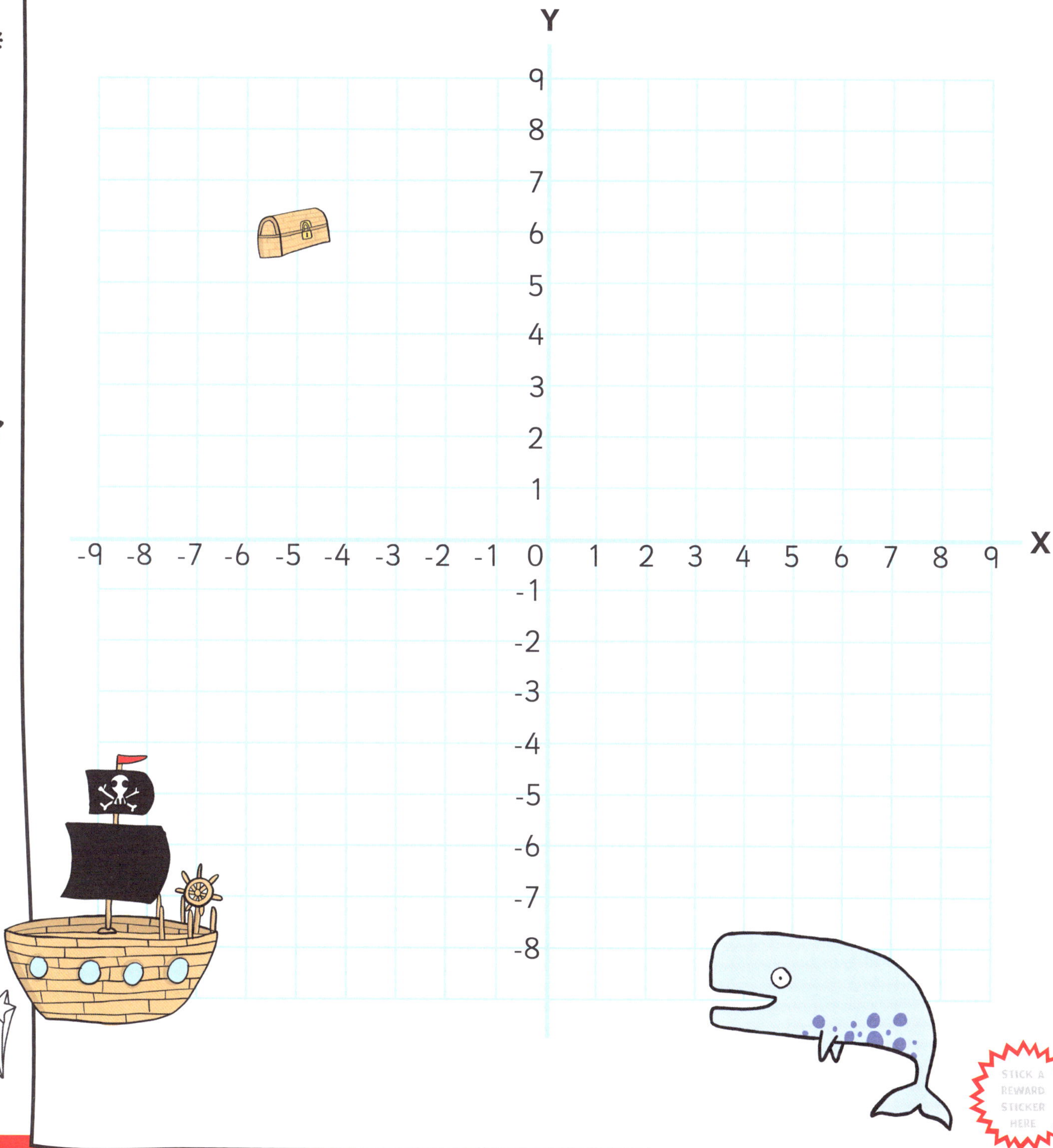

STICK A REWARD STICKER HERE

Answers on page 32

Polygons

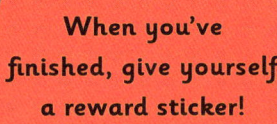

When you've finished, give yourself a reward sticker!

The shapes below are regular or irregular polygons. Label each one using a sticker from the sticker sheet. Write the name of the regular polygons underneath. The first one has been done for you.

regular

square

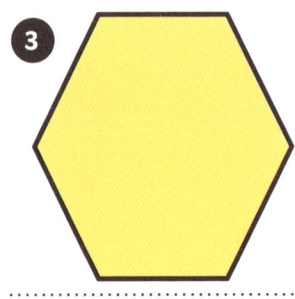

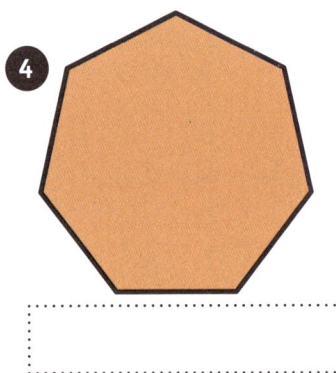

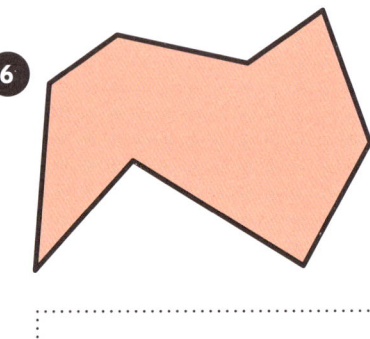

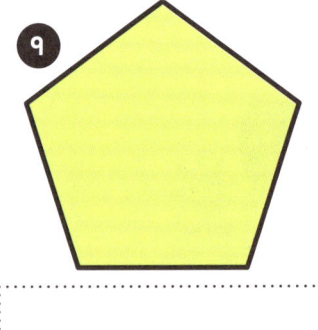

Answers on page 32

Regular or irregular?

Draw two regular polygons. How do you know they are regular? Write a reason on the dotted lines.

....

....

Draw two irregular polygons. How do you know they are irregular? Write a reason on the dotted lines.

....

....

Translation

Translation is when a shape is moved from its original position to a new position, without turning or rotating.

 For example, the shape below has moved 4 squares to the right.

In the grid below, using the stickers on your sticker sheet, move the purple shape 5 squares down, then move the pink shape 2 squares to the left and 4 squares up.

Answers on page 32

Sequences

Fill in the blanks in the number sequences below. Write the rule underneath each one. The first rule has been done for you.

10   20   ☐   40   50   60   70   ☐   90   100   ☐   120

Add 10 each time.

5   10   15   20   ☐   30   35   ☐   45   ☐   ☐   60

3   6   9   12   15   ☐   21   ☐   27   ☐   33   ☐

1   2   4   7   11   ☐   22   29   37   46   ☐   ☐

Write out two of your own number sequences and write the rule underneath each one.

☐ ☐ ☐ ☐ ☐ ☐ ☐ ☐

☐ ☐ ☐ ☐ ☐ ☐ ☐ ☐

Answers on page 32

Adding fractions

When you've finished, give yourself a reward sticker!

Llama and his friends have ordered three pizzas for their weekend treat. Each pizza has 8 slices.

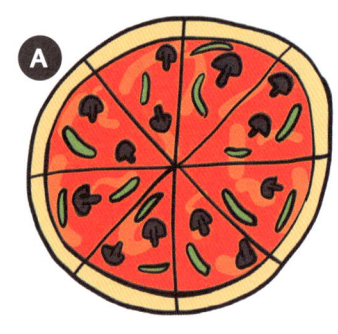 A
 B
 C

"Waiter, will my pizza be long?"
"No, sir. It will be round!"

They eat $\frac{1}{2}$ of Pizza A, $\frac{3}{4}$ of Pizza B and $\frac{1}{8}$ of Pizza C. Place the correct number of pizza slice stickers in the box to show how many slices they have got left over.

Fill in the missing denominators and numerators using the stickers on the sticker sheet.

① $\frac{2}{5} + \frac{1}{5} = \frac{\Box}{5}$

② $\frac{11}{13} + \frac{1}{13} = \frac{\Box}{\Box}$

③ $\frac{2}{10} + \frac{\Box}{10} = \frac{8}{10}$

④ $\frac{21}{37} + \frac{\Box}{37} = \frac{29}{\Box}$

⑤ $\frac{9}{20} + \frac{3}{\Box} = \frac{\Box}{20}$

⑥ $\frac{19}{23} + \frac{2}{\Box} = \frac{\Box}{23}$

STICK A REWARD STICKER HERE

Answers on page 32

Subtracting fractions

The following weekend, Llama and his friends take a homemade cake to a charity bake sale. The cake is split into 12 slices, and they sell 8 slices. What fraction of the cake is left? Show your working out.

....

....

....

The following day, Llama takes two cakes into another school bake sale. One is split into 20 slices and they sell 16. The other is split into 10 slices and they sell 8. What fraction of each cake is left? Use simplified fractions.

....

....

....

Fill in the missing denominators and numerators using the stickers on the sticker sheet.

① $\dfrac{4}{5} - \dfrac{1}{5} = \dfrac{\Box}{5}$

② $\dfrac{12}{13} - \dfrac{5}{13} = \dfrac{\Box}{\Box}$

③ $\dfrac{4}{10} - \dfrac{\Box}{10} = \dfrac{3}{10}$

④ $\dfrac{17}{18} - \dfrac{10}{18} = \dfrac{\Box}{\Box}$

⑤ $\dfrac{9}{25} - \dfrac{3}{\Box} = \dfrac{\Box}{25}$

⑥ $\dfrac{19}{23} - \dfrac{2}{\Box} = \dfrac{\Box}{23}$

Answers on page 32

Simplifying fractions

Simplify the fractions below to their simplest form.

1. $\dfrac{4}{10}$ ....

2. $\dfrac{2}{40}$ ....

3. $\dfrac{10}{100}$ ....

4. $\dfrac{30}{90}$ ....

Add the following fractions, then simplify the answer to its simplest form.

5. $\dfrac{4}{20} + \dfrac{8}{20} =$ ....

6. $\dfrac{3}{10} + \dfrac{2}{10} =$ ....

Answers on page 32

Ordering fractions

Simplify the fractions below so that they all have 10 as their denominator.

1. $\dfrac{80}{100}$ ....

2. $\dfrac{20}{100}$ ....

3. $\dfrac{60}{100}$ ....

4. $\dfrac{10}{100}$ ....

What does a lion do on a canoe? Use his roar!

5. $\dfrac{50}{100}$ ....

Now write the simplified fractions from smallest to largest in the boxes below.

Answers on page 32

27

Radius

A circle has a radius, diameter and circumference.
The radius and diameter can be measured with a ruler.

The radius is the distance halfway across a circle.
Can you tick the image below that correctly shows the radius?

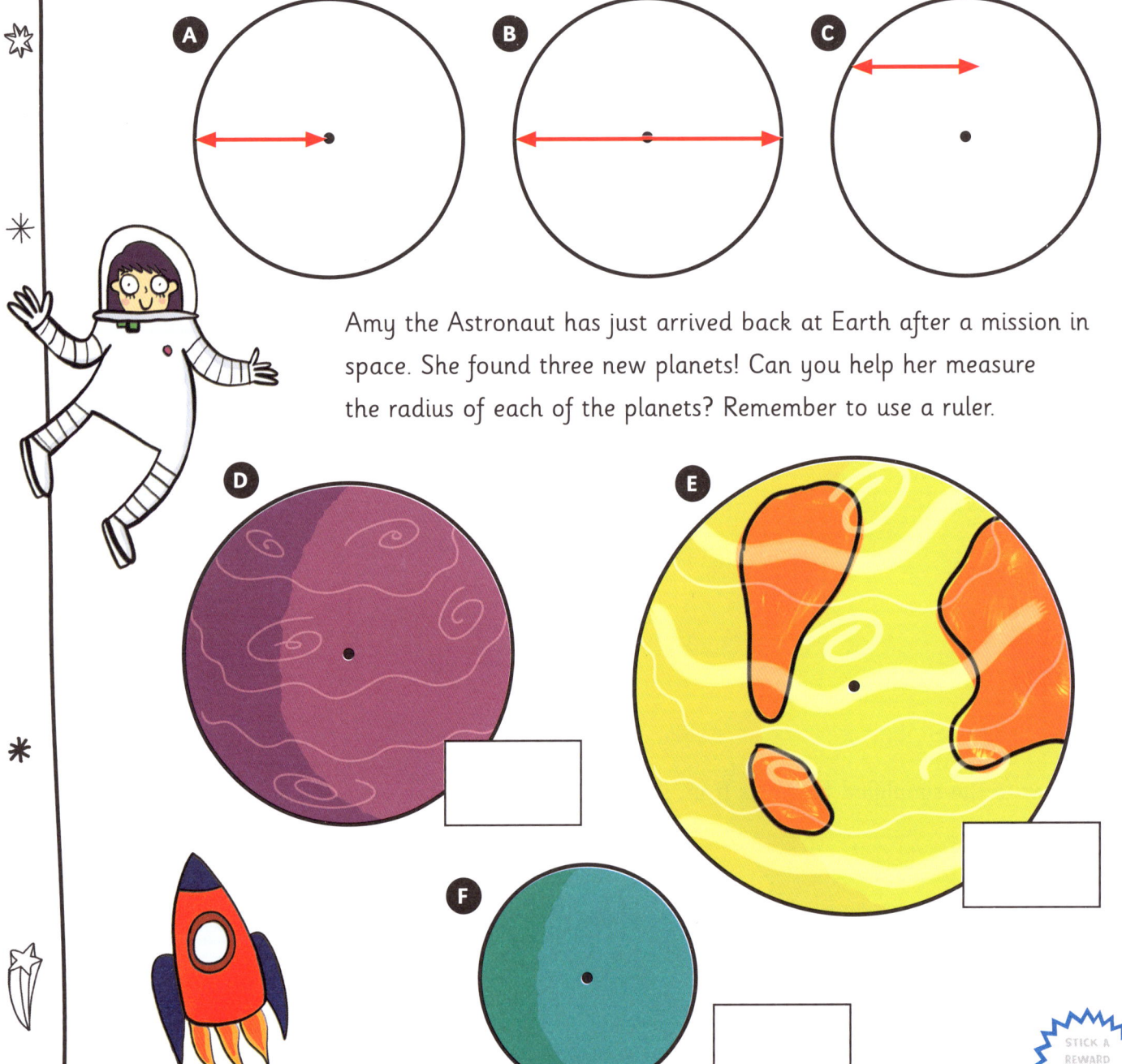

Amy the Astronaut has just arrived back at Earth after a mission in space. She found three new planets! Can you help her measure the radius of each of the planets? Remember to use a ruler.

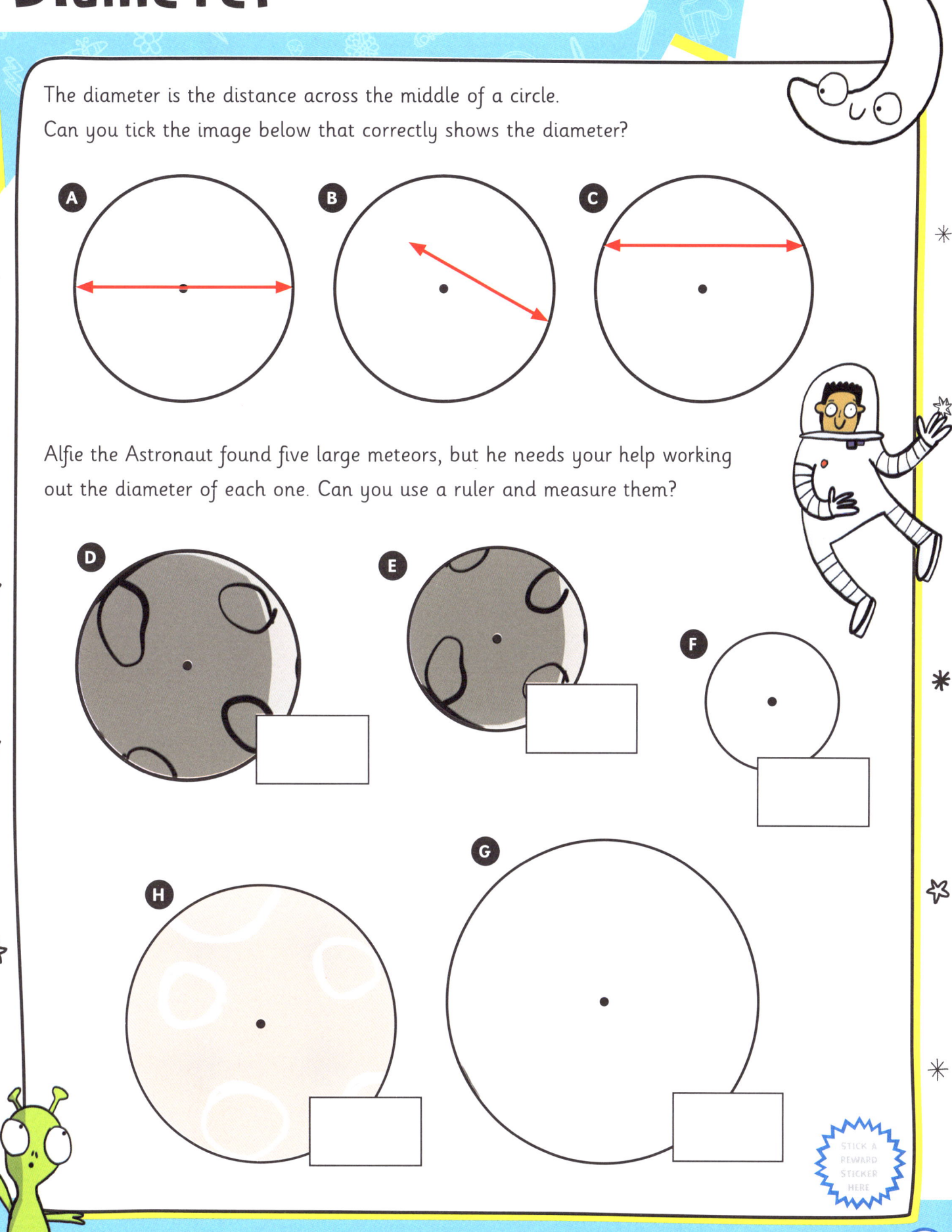

Circumference

The circumference is the distance all the way around a circle.
Can you tick the image below that correctly shows the circumference?

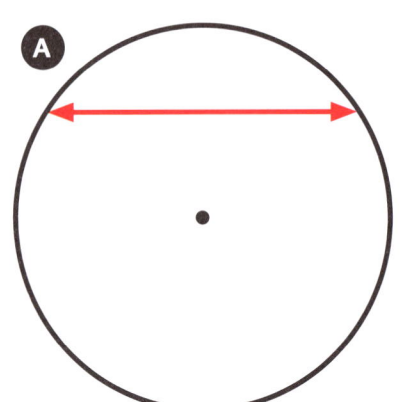
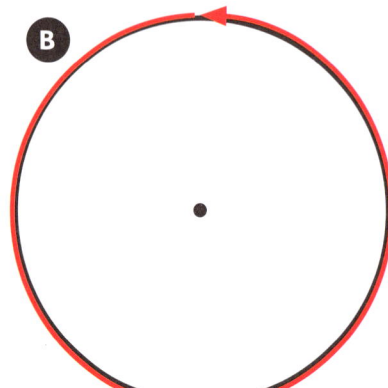
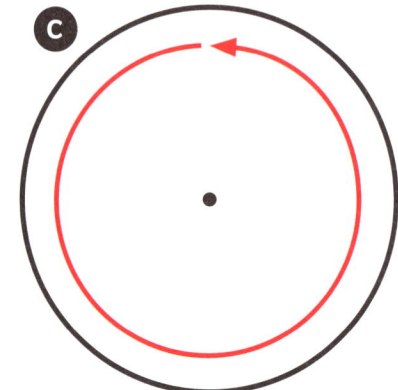

Amy also found some moons on her space mission. Can you use the stickers on the sticker sheet to put them in order from smallest circumference to largest circumference? The stickers are not to scale.

Moon A 24.5 km circumference

Moon B 57.1 km circumference

Moon C 21.09 km circumference

Moon D 21.9 km circumference

Moon E 57.7 km circumference

Answers on page 32

Answers

Page 2: Multiplication
1. 4 **2.** 12 **3.** 10 **4.** 8 **5.** 0 **6.** 56 **7.** 90 **8.** 44 **9.** 72 **10.** 2842 **11.** 1254 **12.** 7055

Page 3: Division
1. 1 **2.** 2 **3.** 10 **4.** 4 **5.** 6 **6.** 4 **7.** 6 **8.** 6 **9.** 8 **10.** 50 **11.** 39 **12.** 57 **13.** 19

Page 4: Alien addition
1. 120 + 140 = 260 **2.** 175 + 122 = 297 **3.** 505 + 101 = 606 **4.** 1000 + 1458 = 2458
5. 160 **6.** 246 **7.** 816 **8.** 212 **9.** 1073 **10.** 756 **11.** 751 **12.** 901

Page 5: Super subtraction
Bananas = 2, Pizza = 0, Apples = 7, Ice cream = 1, Cherries = 13, Burgers = 4, Cake = 1.
59 – 3 – 9 – 19 – 1 = 27. 27 biscuits are left.

Page 6: Perimeter
1. 30 m / 3000 cm **2.** 30 m / 3000 cm **3.** 24 m / 2400 cm **4.** 22 m / 2200 cm
5. 34 m / 3400 cm. Sam will need 70 fence sections for all 5 fields.

Page 7: Area
1. 35 m² **2.** 12 m² **3.** 54 m² **4.** 18 m² **5.** 20 m². Orange fish = pond 2. Yellow fish = pond 3.

Page 8: Square numbers
5^2 5 x 5 = 25 6^2 6 x 6 = 36 8^2 8 x 8 = 64 10^2 10 x 10 = 100   **1.** T. rex is correct because 2 x 2 = 4.
2. Triceratops has calculated 11 + 11 but should have calculated 11 x 11 = 121. **3.** Diplodocus is correct because 7 x 7 = 49.

Page 9: Cube numbers
4^3 = 64 5^3 = 125 7^3 = 343 10^3 = 1000
1. Diplodocus is correct. **2.** He's done 9 x 3 rather than 9 x 9 x 9 = 729. **3.** 12 x 12 x 12 = 1728

Page 10: Rounding decimals
1. 5.39 = 5 **2.** 5.81 = 6 **3.** 2.05 = 2 **4.** 9.92 = 10 **5.** 4.54 = 4.5
6. 2.11 = 2.1 **7.** 9.56 = 9.6 **8.** 8.32 = 8.3 **9.** 3.92 = 3.9 **10.** 2.1, 3.9, 4.5, 8.3, 9.6

Page 11: Percentages
1. 50% **2.** 0.3 **3.** 75% **4.** 0.2 **5.** 50% **6.** 25% **7.** 80%

Page 12: Multiplication
1. 46 **2.** 460 **3.** 880 **4.** 930 **5.** 890 **6.** 37.5 **7.** 485 **8.** 91.2 **9.** 555

Page 13: Division
1. 46 **2.** 4.6 **3.** 4.6 **4.** 9.3 **5.** 8.5 **6.** 37.5 **7.** 4.85 **8.** 91 **9.** 5.55

Page 14: Rounding whole numbers
1. 130 **2.** 380 **3.** 4990 **4.** 1120 **5.** 500 **6.** 500 **7.** 400 **8.** 100 **9.** 5000 **10.** 4000 **11.** 3000 **12.** 6000

Page 15: Roman numerals
2. 20 = XX = twenty   **3.** 50 = L = fifty   **4.** 100 = C = one hundred   **5.** 150 = CL = one hundred and fifty
6. 200 = CC = two hundred **7.** 230 = CCXXX = two hundred and thirty **8.** 265 = CCLXV = two hundred and sixty-five
9. 380 = CCCLXXX = three hundred and eighty   **10.** 550 = DL = five hundred and fifty

Answers

Page 16: Angles in triangles

1. 35° **2.** 85° **3.** 25°

Page 17: Missing angles
1. 60° **2.** 100° **3.** 80° **4.** 180° **5.** 150°

Page 18: Reading scales

1. 25 °C **2.** 2 °C **3.** 0 °C **4.** 15 °C **5.** 10 °C **6.** 40 °C

Page 19: Pirate coordinates

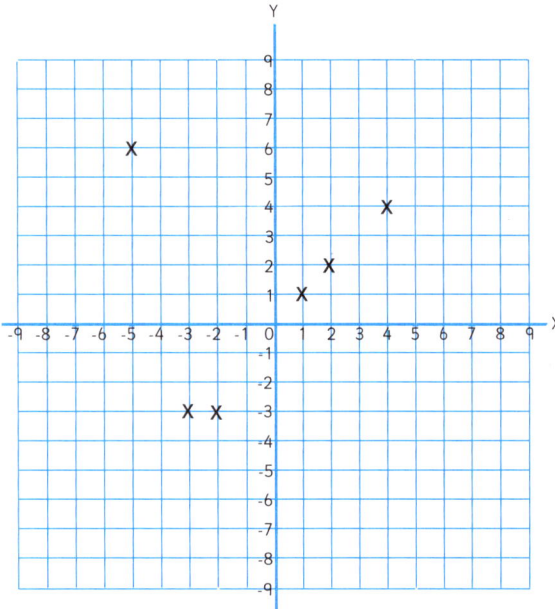

Page 20: Polygons
1. regular, square **2.** irregular **3.** regular, hexagon
4. regular, heptagon **5.** irregular **6.** irregular **7.** regular, octagon
8. irregular **9.** regular, pentagon

Page 22: Translation

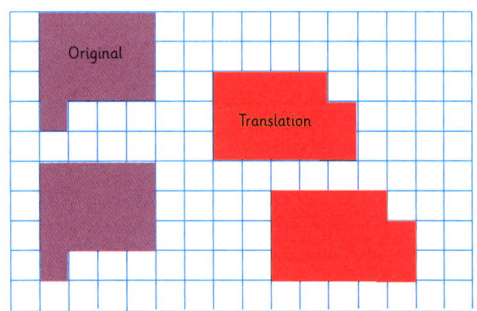

Page 23: Sequences
10 20 **30** 40 50 60 70 **80** 90 100 **110** 120 (add 10 each time)
5 10 15 20 **25** 30 35 **40** 45 **50 55** 60 (add 5 each time)
3 6 9 12 15 **18** 21 **24** 27 **30** 33 **36** (add 3 each time)
1 2 4 7 11 **16** 22 29 37 46 **56 67** (add 1, then add 2, then add 3, and so on, increasing by 1 each time)

Page 24: Adding fractions
Pizza A has 4 slices left. **Pizza B** has 2 slices left. **Pizza C** has 7 slices left. Therefore, there should be 13 pizza slice stickers on the plate.

1. $\frac{2}{5} + \frac{1}{5} = \frac{3}{5}$ **2.** $\frac{11}{13} + \frac{1}{13} = \frac{12}{13}$ **3.** $\frac{2}{10} + \frac{6}{10} = \frac{8}{10}$
4. $\frac{21}{37} + \frac{8}{37} = \frac{29}{37}$ **5.** $\frac{9}{20} + \frac{3}{20} = \frac{12}{20}$ **6.** $\frac{19}{23} + \frac{2}{23} = \frac{21}{23}$

Page 25: Subtracting fractions

12 − 8 = 4 slices left which is $\frac{4}{12} = \frac{1}{3}$. 20 − 16 = 4 which is $\frac{4}{20}$. 10 − 8 = 2 which is $\frac{2}{10}$.
These two fractions simplified are $\frac{1}{5}$ and $\frac{1}{5}$.

1. $\frac{4}{5} - \frac{1}{5} = \frac{3}{5}$ **2.** $\frac{12}{13} - \frac{5}{13} = \frac{7}{13}$ **3.** $\frac{4}{10} - \frac{1}{10} = \frac{3}{10}$
4. $\frac{17}{18} - \frac{10}{18} = \frac{7}{18}$ **5.** $\frac{9}{25} - \frac{3}{25} = \frac{6}{25}$ **6.** $\frac{19}{23} - \frac{2}{23} = \frac{17}{23}$

Page 26: Simplifying fractions
1. $\frac{2}{5}$ **2.** $\frac{1}{20}$ **3.** $\frac{1}{10}$ **4.** $\frac{1}{3}$ **5.** $\frac{3}{5}$ **6.** $\frac{1}{2}$

Page 27: Ordering fractions
1. $\frac{8}{10}$ **2.** $\frac{2}{10}$ **3.** $\frac{6}{10}$ **4.** $\frac{1}{10}$ **5.** $\frac{5}{10}$

In order:
$\frac{1}{10}$ $\frac{2}{10}$ $\frac{5}{10}$ $\frac{6}{10}$ $\frac{8}{10}$

Page 28: Radius
Circle A is correct. **D.** 3 cm (30 mm) **E.** 4 cm (40 mm)
F. 2 cm (20 mm)

Page 29: Diameter
Circle A is correct. **D.** 5 cm (50 mm) **E.** 4 cm (40 mm)
F. 3 cm (30 mm) **G.** 7 cm (70 mm) **H.** 6 cm (60 mm)

Page 30: Circumference
Circle B is correct.
Correct order is: Moon C, Moon D, Moon A, Moon B, Moon E.

32

Help with HOMEWORK

9+

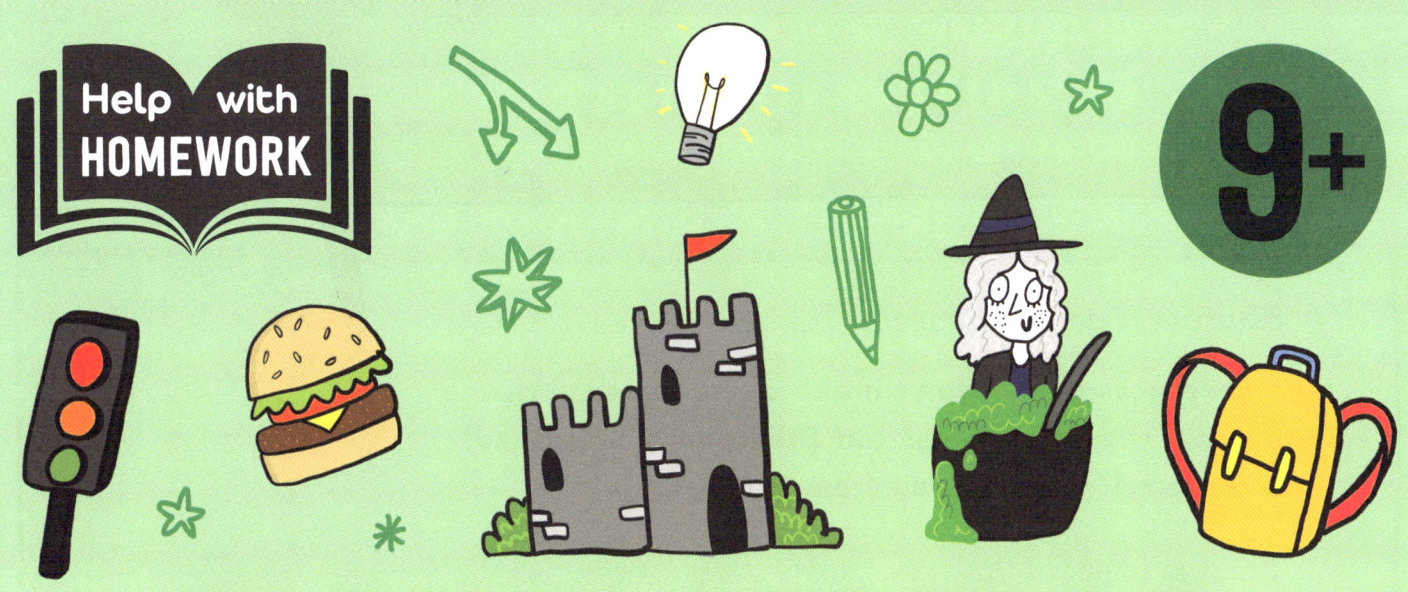

ENGLISH ESSENTIALS

Practise the skills you need for Key Stage 2 English

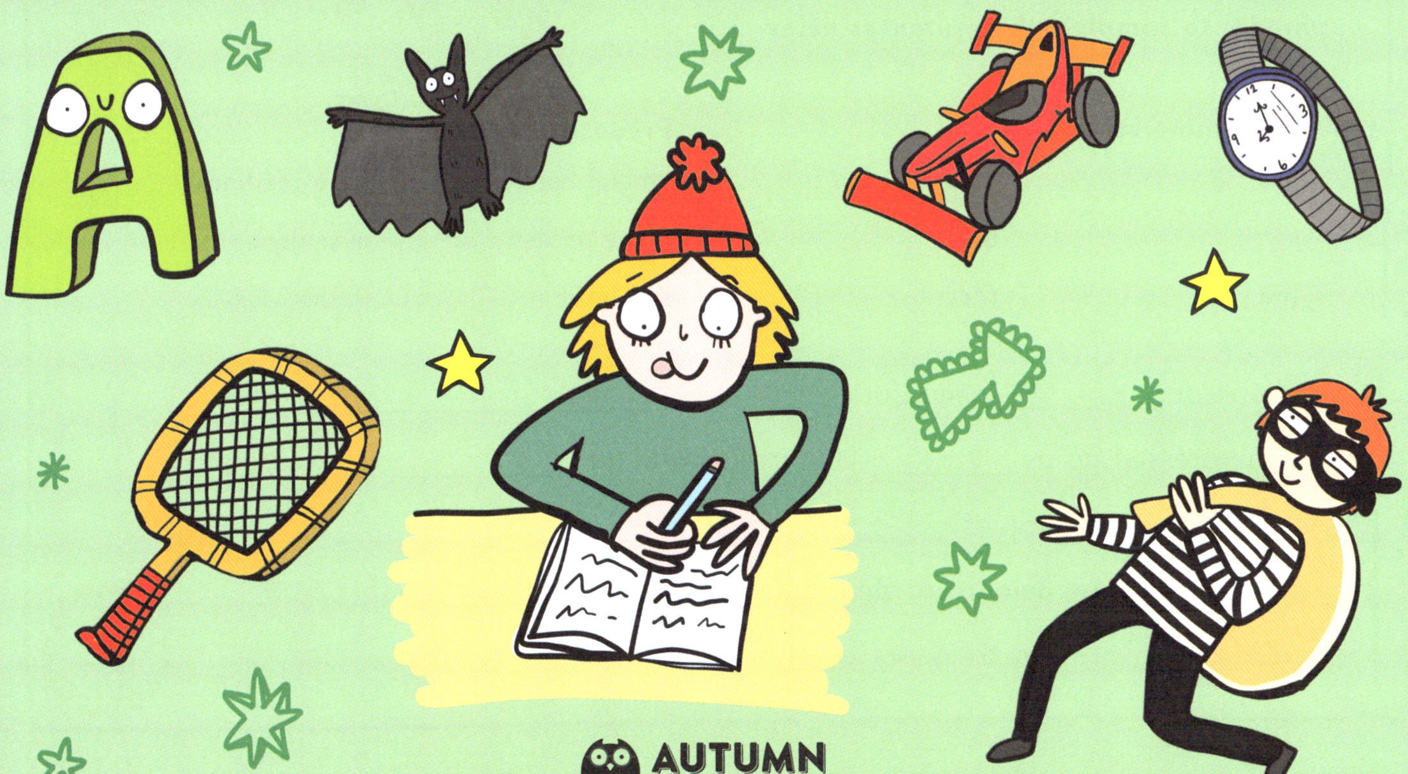

AUTUMN PUBLISHING

Know your nouns

A **noun** is a person, place or thing.

The sentences below don't make sense because the nouns are incorrect. Cross out the noun (underlined) and replace it with a noun from the box.

1. I hurt my <u>hair</u>. _____
2. The <u>river</u> is still wet. _____
3. Don't touch the <u>clouds</u>! _____
4. Red is my favourite <u>dish</u>. _____
5. Can I have a <u>lion</u>? _____
6. Let's go for a <u>sky</u>. _____

Nouns:
walk   exhibits   paint
colour   biscuit   knee

Get it?
The word 'walk' can be a noun or a verb depending on how it is used in the sentence. E.g. 'a walk' is a noun but 'he walks' is a verb. If you can write 'a' or 'an' before the word, it is usually a noun.

Noun phrases include a noun, plus any other words that modify (describe) the noun. You can also use preposition phrases to describe a noun.

Use the determiners and preposition phrases to complete the sentences below.

Determiners:
her   those
some   three
the   that

Preposition phrases:
around the corner   from the book
in the garden   over there
on platform 5   in the basket

1. Look at _____ beautiful cherry tree _____ .
2. She dressed up as _____ favourite character _____ .
3. I like _____ puppies _____ .
4. The pencil case belongs to Ben. It's _____ .
5. Catch _____ next train _____ .

Answers on page 31

Expanded noun phrases

Preposition phrases can tell you more about a noun, such as where it is or when it is.

For example: **the old, stone wall at the end of the garden**.

The words 'old' and 'stone' are adjectives describing the wall. The phrase 'at the end of the garden' is a prepositional phrase telling you where the wall is.

To complete the table below, fill in the blank spaces by choosing adjectives, nouns and preposition phrases to make expanded noun phrases.

Adjectives:	Noun:	Preposition phrase:
the warm, bright	sun	in the morning
	clown	with a red nose
a ferocious	dog	
those terrifying, dark		at midnight
		over the hills

Create some of your own in the table below.

Adjectives:	Noun:	Preposition phrase:

Adding adjectives

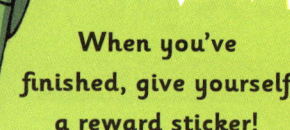

When you've finished, give yourself a reward sticker!

An adjective is a describing word that tells you more about a noun.
For example, a building… a **new** building… a **wonderful**, **new** building.

Underline the adjectives in the sentences below.

1. The clever detective caught the notorious thief.
2. Spectacular fireworks lit up the night sky.
3. A gigantic, hairy spider sat beside the nervous boy.

Get it?
Adding adjectives before nouns will make your writing more interesting and informative for the reader.

Select the most appropriate adjectives from the box on the right to describe each noun in these sentences. Then write the new sentences on the lines below.

Adjectives:
comfortable
terrified
delicious
excitable
flowing
Japanese

4. The dog chased the cat.

   _____

5. We had a meal in a restaurant.

   _____

6. She wore a dress and shoes.

   _____

Answers on page 31

Perfect your pronouns

Pronouns are useful because they can be used instead of repeating a noun. Pronouns can also be used to link sentences.

Replace the nouns (underlined below) with personal pronouns from the box.

1. The reds beat the blues. <u>The reds</u> won by two points. _____
2. Jack loved the film when <u>Jack</u> saw <u>the film</u>. _____
3. Bella is in my class. Do you know <u>Bella</u>? _____
4. Our neighbours are friendly when you get to know <u>our neighbours</u>. _____

Personal pronouns:

I	you
we / us	it
him / her	he / she
they / them	

Possessive pronouns tell you who owns something, e.g. the bike belongs to Tom. It's **his**.

Choose a possessive pronoun from the box to complete each of the following sentences:

1. The ice cream belongs to Harpreet. It's _____ .
2. The snake belongs to us. It's _____ .
3. The hat belongs to you. It's _____ .
4. The car belongs to them. It's _____ .

Possessive pronouns:

ours	yours
mine	theirs
his	its
hers	

5. The pencil case belongs to Ben. It's _____ .
6. The dog belongs to us. It's _____ .
7. The book belongs to you. It's _____ .
8. The ball belongs to me. It's _____ .

Verbs and adverbs

A **verb** is a doing word. It tells us about the action taking place.
Which of these sentences sounds the most interesting?

WEAK VERB
1. The boy **went** across the field.

BETTER VERB
2. The boy **ran** across the field.

VERB + ADVERB
3. The boy **ran quickly** across the field.*

STRONG VERB
4. The boy **sprinted** across the field.

Get it?
The sentence with the strong verb is the most interesting. It gives the reader a clear picture of the action. One strong word is better than lots of weak words.

*If the verb is not very strong, then an adverb is needed, e.g. **ran quickly**. You wouldn't need to add **quickly** after sprinted because **sprinted** is strong enough to convey the action.

Choose the most appropriate strong verbs to complete the sentences below.

1. The racecar **dawdled / trundled / screeched** around the track.

2. The mouse **meandered / strolled / scampered** under the sofa.

3. The waves **crashed / trickled / dribbled** onto the rocks.

4. The girl **hollered / whispered / shouted** the secret to her friend.

5. The boy **stomped / clattered / crept** through the spooky house.

Answers on page 31

An **adverb** tells us more about a verb. It tells us **how**, **when** or **where** the action of the verb takes place, e.g. the boy ran **quickly**.

When you've finished, give yourself a reward sticker!

Write an adverb after these verbs. Choose from the box or use your own.

1. He looked _____ at his opponent.
2. They spoke _____ on the phone.
3. She sang _____ into the microphone.
4. The wind blew _____ .
5. The volcano erupted _____ .

Adverbs:

fiercely	quietly
angrily	jokingly
outside	still
kindly	loudly
suddenly	gently

Some adverbs are used to show how possible or certain things can be.

For example:

You **definitely** should do your homework before athletics.

There are some examples of adverbs for "possibility" in the box to the right.

Adverbs for possibility:

possibly

surely

perhaps

mostly

definitely

Choose the most appropriate adverbs from the box for the sentences below:

1. It could _____ snow tomorrow.
2. _____ you could come swimming with me on Saturday.
3. It _____ will get dark tonight.

Get it?
An adverb can change the meaning of the verb. For example, someone can look **suspiciously** or move **curiously** around a room.

Answers on page 31

Adverbial phrases

Adverbial phrases modify a verb. They do the same job as an adverb but are a group of words. An adverbial phrase gives us more information about the time, place and manner of the action being described.

For example:

How - the boy ran **with haste.**

When - the sun set **after tea.**

Where - the children played **behind the wall.**

Below is a newspaper report about a burglar who broke into a jewellery shop. Underline the adverbial phrases in the report:

Yesterday, at 11:58pm, a burglar broke into a jewellery shop on John Street.

It is claimed that the criminal threw a large rock through the front window and robbed the shop within minutes.

The jeweller, who lived above the shop, awoke to the sound of the shop alarm going off below his flat. By the time he ran downstairs, the burglar had escaped down the street, carrying a large bag of expensive digital watches.

The suspect has not yet been found.

ADVERBIAL PHRASES TELL US HOW, WHEN AND WHERE AN ACTION TOOK PLACE.

Answers on page 31

Playing with words

Similes are when you describe something as being <u>like</u> something else.

For example, the rocks were jagged **like shark's teeth**.

Make up some of your own similes to complete these descriptions:

1. The crashing waves were like _____

2. The hot sun was like _____

3. The autumn leaves were like _____

4. The tiger's eyes were like _____

Metaphors are when you say that something <u>is</u> something else.

For example, she's a clown! (She is always joking.)

Choose a metaphor from the box on the right to describe these people or things.

Metaphors:

A snake in the grass   A ray of sunshine

A fly in the ointment   A night owl

1. Someone who is always smiling. _____

2. Someone who is sneaky. _____

3. Someone who stays up late. _____

Onomatopoeia is a word that sounds like the thing it is describing.

Buzz!   Crash!   Pop!   Glug!   Squelch!   Plop!   Squeak!

Write some more examples of onomatopoeia:

_____

_____

_____

Answers on page 31

Full stops and capitals

We put a **full stop** (.) at the end of a main clause.
New sentences always start with a capital letter.

When you've finished, give yourself a reward sticker!

Read the following passage and add full stops in the right place.

i wake up each morning before the alarm i wait for it to ring on the dot of seven and then i get up however today was going to be different i didn't wake up the alarm didn't ring this difference would change my life forever

Go back to the same passage above and add capital letters for the pronoun 'I', and for the start of each sentence.

Now check against the following text:

I wake up each morning before the alarm. I wait for it to ring on the dot of seven and then I get up. However today was going to be different. I didn't wake up. The alarm didn't ring. This difference would change my life forever.

How did you score? Give yourself one point for each correct full stop and capital letter.

My score: _____

STICK A REWARD STICKER HERE

Answers on page 31

Semicolons and colons

A **semicolon** (;) joins parts of a sentence where there are closely connected ideas.

For example:

I didn't wake up; the alarm didn't ring.

Write a sentence that contains a semicolon. Use it to link your ideas together.

_____

Colons (:) appear at the start of a list or just before an explanation.

For example:

To make my favourite sandwich, you will need: bread, margarine, tuna and cucumber. Here's why I like it so much: it's delicious.

If you are writing a complicated list, you can use semicolons to help you separate the items.

For example:

To make my favourite sandwich, you will need: wholemeal or brown bread, cut into two slices; thinly-sliced cucumber; drained tuna flakes; and reduced-fat, low-salt margarine.

Write a list of ingredients (starting with a colon) for your favourite sandwich. Add commas and/or semicolons to separate items in the list.

For my favourite sandwich, you will need

_____

How to use apostrophes

Apostrophes have two important jobs:

1. An apostrophe tells you who owns what – this is called **possession**.
   For example, the shark's teeth (the teeth belonging to the shark).

2. An apostrophe tells you which words are shortened – this is called **contraction**.
   For example, It's a shark! (It is a shark!)

Write a phrase containing a possessive apostrophe for each of the statements below.

The first one has been done for you.

1. the desk belonging to the teacher   the teacher's desk
2. the purse belonging to Mum   _____
3. the studio belonging to the artist   _____
4. the whiskers belonging to the cat   _____

If the noun is a plural ending in 's', the apostrophe goes at the end.

Write a phrase containing a plural possessive apostrophe for the statements below.

The first one has been done for you.

1. the dog belonging to the girls   the girls' dog
2. the car belonging to the family   _____
3. the changing room belonging to the players _____
4. the jobs belonging to the people   _____
5. the toys belonging to the babies   _____

Answers on page 31

Get it?

If a plural noun doesn't end in **s**, add **'s** to show possession. For example we write: **the children's school** (not the childrens' school).

Apostrophes are also used when you want to shorten words or phrases. The apostrophe replaces the missing letters.

Learn these contractions:

I am – **I'm**
he is / she is – **he's / she's**
it is – **it's**
you are – **you're**
they are – **they're**
we are – **we're**

do not – **don't**
did not – **didn't**
does not – **doesn't**
cannot – **can't**
could not – **couldn't**
would not – **wouldn't**

IT'S FUN TO SPLASH IN PUDDLES!

Use an apostrophe to shorten words in each of the sentences below.

The first one has been done for you.

1. We cannot go yet.   We can't go yet.
2. She would have liked the taste. _____
3. The dog does not bite. _____
4. The car should have started. _____
5. It is not fair! _____

HOW DO YOU STOP A DOG FROM SMELLING?

HOLD ITS NOSE! (NOT: IT'S NOSE!)

Get it?

It's is a contraction that means **It is** or **It has**. Don't use it as a possessive apostrophe.

Speech (Inverted commas for direct speech)

Inverted commas (" ") tell you exactly what words are spoken by the characters in a story.

Get it?
Inverted commas are drawn at the beginning and at the end of direct speech. All other punctuation (including full stops) goes inside them.

Read the story extract and draw inverted commas around the words that are said by the characters.

> I think Dig is sick, said Tom. He won't eat his dinner.
>
> Perhaps he's not hungry, replied Tom's mum.
>
> But he's *always* hungry! said Tom. And it's his favourite: marinated chicken chunks in juicy jelly.

Continue the conversation between Tom and his mum on the lines below. Start a new line for each new speaker. Draw inverted commas around the words that are spoken.

_____

_____

_____

_____

_____

HE'S JUST ATTENTION-SEEKING!

Conversation often has question marks or exclamation marks.

Question marks (?) tell you that a question is being asked.

Exclamation marks (!) show surprise, humour or excitement.

Read the story extract below. Change the punctuation by substituting question marks or exclamation marks where you think they belong.

> "Mum," shouted Tom.
>
> "Now what," said Tom's mum.
>
> "I know why Dig won't eat his dinner," said Tom. "It's a new recipe. They've added vegetables. You know he hates vegetables."

Continue the conversation between Tom and his mum on the lines below. Include inverted commas, question marks and exclamation marks where necessary.

When you've finished, give yourself a reward sticker!

AW, DIDDUMS WON'T EAT HIS VEGETABLES!

Answers on page 31

Clauses and conjunctions

A sentence or a clause has to include a noun and a verb.

For example:
Dig loves chicken.

Dig is a noun and **loves** is a verb.

....

A **conjunction** is a connecting word that links clauses or sentences.

For example:
Dig loves chicken. He hates vegetables.
Dig loves chicken **but** he hates vegetables.

Coordinating conjunctions	Subordinating conjunctions
and	when
but	because
or	if
yet	that
so	while
	although

Use a conjunction from the table to join these sentences together.

1. Dig didn't eat his dinner. Kit ate it instead.

_____

2. Dig and Kit were friends. They were rivals, too.

_____

3. Tom was worried. Dig hadn't eaten his food.

_____

4. Mum wasn't paying attention. She was busy.

_____

Write a sentence of your own using a conjunction.

_____

Reward stickers

Underline the conjunctions in these sentences.

1. I put the dog on the lead and we went out for a walk.
2. It felt cold although it was sunny.
3. We played in the park until it was dark.
4. Mum was cross when I got home late.
5. I missed my programme because it came on earlier than usual.

Write another sentence of your own using a conjunction.

_____

When you've finished, give yourself a reward sticker!

Sometimes we use **connecting adverbs** to link sentences and paragraphs so that our writing 'flows' better.

For example:
We were watching TV. Suddenly, all the lights went out.

Underline the adverbs that connect these sentences.

1. I missed the last five minutes of the film. Consequently, I don't know how it ended!
2. I can come to your house. However, I can't stay for long.
3. Firstly, you mix the butter and the sugar. Next, you add the egg.
4. Dad did the shopping. Meanwhile, Mum was at work.
5. Do your homework now. Later, you can go swimming.

Some connecting adverbs:

later

suddenly

finally

firstly

next

additionally

meanwhile

consequently

Write two sentences of your own and connect them using a connecting adverb.

_____

_____

_____

Get it?

However is a connecting adverb.

Relative clauses

Relative clauses are a type of clause added into a sentence to give more detail about the nouns. They work a bit like adjectives.

Relative clauses begin with a relative pronoun: **who**, **when**, **where**, **which**, **that** or **whose**.

When a relative clause is in the middle of a sentence, commas are used around the clause to mark it.

For example:

The boy, **who walked along the wall**, was good at balancing.

The house, **where my Nan lived**, was the largest on the street.

Sometimes, relative clauses can come at the end of a sentence. When they are at the end of a sentence, a comma is not used.

E.g. I love the food that Dad cooks.

Add a relative clause to the following sentences. Don't forget to add commas!

The friends _____ decided to meet at the park.

Cheetahs _____ can run extremely fast.

The town _____
_____ was difficult to find.

The necklace _____
_____ was very precious.

Parenthesis (using brackets, dashes and commas)

You can use other types of punctuation to mark extra information or relative clauses. As well as commas, you can use brackets and dashes to add extra information.

- Commas work best with relative clauses:

  The bus driver**, who was aged 46,** travelled down the wrong side of the road.

- Brackets are useful when you give a short, succinct version of the information:

  The bus driver **(aged 46)** travelled down the wrong side of the road.

- Dashes are good for informal comments. They are used in texts like emails and diaries:

  The bus driver **– unbelievably –** travelled down the wrong side of the road.

Work out which punctuation works best in the following sentences, then add **brackets**, **dashes** or **commas** into the boxes below.

1. The staircase ☐ 735 steps ☐ winds around the inside of the castle.
2. The Himalayas ☐ where the largest mountain in the world is situated ☐ are in Nepal.
3. The weather ☐ thunder and lightning ☐ spoiled our barbecue.
4. The car ☐ annoyingly ☐ would not start when we needed to get to school.

Prefixes

A **prefix** is a group of letters added to the beginning of a word that changes the word's meaning.

For example, the prefix 'pre' means 'before' (in Latin):
preschool = before school
prehistoric = before history

Add prefixes to these words.

1. 'aqua' (means 'water' in Latin)

   _ _ _ _ rium

   _ _ _ _ tic

   _ _ _ _ _ marine

2. 'viv' (means 'live' in Latin)

   _ _ _ isect

   _ _ _ acious

   _ _ _ id

3. 'geo' (means 'Earth' in Greek)

   _ _ _ metry

   _ _ _ logy

   _ _ _ graphy

4. 'bio' (means 'life' in Greek)

   _ _ _ graphy

   _ _ _ nic

   _ _ _ logical

5. 'oct' (means 'eight' in Greek)

   _ _ _ opus

   _ _ _ agon

   _ _ _ ave

6. 'super' (means 'over' or 'above' in Latin)

   _ _ _ _ _ market

   _ _ _ _ _ sonic

   _ _ _ _ _ visor

Suffixes

A **suffix** is a group of letters added to the end of a word.

Using a suffix can change the tense (from past to present tense and vice versa) or the meaning of a word.

Suffixes:
-en / -ed   -ish   -ation   -less   -ment
-er / -or   -ing   -ful   -ly   -ness

Add suffixes to these words.

1. instruct + or = _____
2. act + or = _____
3. conduct + or = _____
4. hope + less = _____
5. sleep + less = _____
6. rest + less = _____
7. excite + ment = _____
8. move + ment = _____
9. agree + ment = _____
10. immediate + ly = _____
11. sudden + ly = _____
12. extreme + ly = _____

When the root word ends in a vowel and you want to add a suffix that starts with a vowel, you drop one of the vowels.

Try these:

1. spice + ed = _____
2. care + ing = _____
3. late + er = _____

Get it?
The vowels are: **a, e, i, o, u.** The other letters in the alphabet are called consonants.

Double the consonant when there is a single vowel before a single consonant, e.g. sit + ing = sitting.

Try these:

4. big + est = _____
5. swim + ing = _____
6. stop + ed = _____

Learn these:
beauty + ful = beautiful
happy + ness = happiness

Answers on page 32

Different kinds of writing

Diaries, letters and autobiographies are written in the **first person** using the pronouns **I**, **my**, **mine** and **we**.

Underline the first-person pronouns in this diary extract:

> Somehow I knew that today was going to be special, even though it started off like every other day – I was going to be late for school again!

Instructions and advertisements are written in the **second person** using the pronouns **you** and **your**.

Underline the second-person pronouns in this instruction text:

> To make chocolate brownies you need: flour, cocoa powder, eggs, butter and milk. But first, you need to find an adult to help you!

Novels, stories, information books and newspaper reports are often written in the **third person** using the pronouns **he**, **she**, **it** and **they**.

Underline the third-person pronouns in this story extract:

> "I'm so happy!" she said. "I want to thank everyone who voted for me!" They cheered enthusiastically as she lifted the winner's trophy.

Write three pieces of text – one in the first person, one in the second person and one in the third person.

LOOK FOR EXAMPLES IN BOOKS TO HELP YOU.

First person

_____
_____
_____
_____

Second person

_____
_____
_____
_____

Third person

_____
_____
_____
_____

Get it?

There are two main types of writing. **Fiction** is not true; it is made up by the storyteller. **Non-fiction** is true; it is writing based on facts and real events.

Answers on page 32

Writing stories (fiction)

> When you write a story, the first thing you need to decide on is where and when the action takes place – this is called the **setting**.

Writers often set their stories in places that are familiar to them, for example school, home, neighbourhood, workplace or somewhere they went on holiday.

Possible settings:

new school	raging river	remote rainforest
busy airport	noisy campsite	space station

Choose one of these settings and write notes on the mind map below about the things you can see, hear, touch, taste and smell.

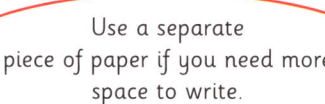
Use a separate piece of paper if you need more space to write.

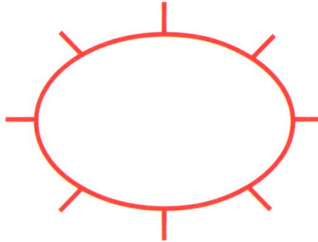

Decide whether the setting is in the past, present or future.

Characters are essential to tell the story.

Any characters you invent should have a clear purpose in the story and a distinct personality. They might be unusual in some way, e.g. in the way they dress or speak.

Match the following characters to the settings in the box above.
There are no right or wrong answers.

Polly Phonic – friendly, talkative   **Venus Strange** – clever, mysterious

Miss McEvil – controlling, ambitious   **Gazza Green** – loud, outdoorsy-type

Ace Bravado – daredevil, adventure seeker   **Leif Biome** – wacky, curious nature

Now choose one of these characters and invent others to match your chosen setting. Make up names and character descriptions. Use a separate piece of paper for this work.

STICK A REWARD STICKER HERE

All stories must have a **plot** or **theme** – this is what the story is about and what the characters do.

Here are some popular story ideas:

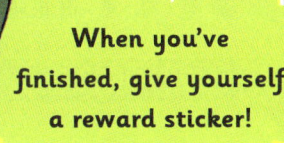

When you've finished, give yourself a reward sticker!

Possible plots:
good versus evil   a misunderstanding   a comedy
something is lost or stolen   journey of discovery   friendship theme

Choose a plot to match your setting and characters.

Write a story plan in five paragraphs:

Beginning – introduce your setting and characters

_____
_____

Build up – things start to happen and the plot develops

_____
_____

Crisis – a series of things go wrong, leading to a crisis

_____
_____

Solution – the characters manage to sort out the problem

_____
_____

Ending – the characters reflect on what has happened or changed

_____
_____

Now you are ready to write out your story in full! Use a separate piece of paper for this.

Writing non-fiction

When you've finished, give yourself a reward sticker!

Reports, recounts, instructions and discussions are examples of **non-fiction** writing.

Reports – writing about the facts known on a given topic. Use specialist vocabulary and define the terms used. Use a formal style in present tense. Illustrate with diagrams or pictures.

Recounts – writing about an event you have witnessed or an experience you have had. Use pronouns: I, we, he, she, they. Write in the past tense using powerful verbs. Use time connectives such as: then, when, later, next, eventually.

Instructions – writing about how to do something. Include lists of materials needed. Write a clear sequence of steps. Use verbs. For example: cut, mix, stir, place. Use time connectives and pronouns such as you and your.

Discussions – writing about a topic to provide a balanced viewpoint or discussion. Write the points 'for' and 'against', using evidence to back up the argument. Use present tense and emotional language to engage with the reader. Reach a conclusion at the end.

Read the following report text:

Fast Cats

The cheetah is the fastest land animal. Cheetahs can reach speeds of up to 70 miles per hour (113 kph). They can accelerate faster than the average car: 0-60 miles per hour (0-97 kph) in only 3 seconds!

Their long legs and athletic bodies are built for fast acceleration. Wildebeest, their prey, are fast, too, but they are slower to accelerate. The cheetah, however, can't maintain this speed over long distances so sometimes the wildebeest manage to outrun them.

Larger cats such as leopards and tigers are slower because their bulkier bodies have to use more muscle and energy to propel them forwards. They can reach up to 35-40 miles per hour (56-65 kph) in short bursts.

Domestic cats can run up to 30 miles per hour (48 kph). They have lost some of their speed because they no longer need to chase their dinner!

Now answer these questions in complete sentences:

1. What makes the cheetah so fast?

   _____

   _____

2. Is the cheetah faster than the average car?

   _____

   _____

3. How does the wildebeest manage to outrun the cheetah?

   _____

   _____

4. Why have domestic cats lost some of their speed?

   _____

   _____

5. What tense (past, present or future) is the text written in?

   _____

   _____

Answers on page 32

A discussion

Read the following discussion text:

Do dogs make good pets?

People have kept dogs as pets for hundreds of years. Dogs can be easily house-trained to live in our homes. They form loyal and protective bonds with their owners and for older people who live alone, a dog can provide companionship. Studies have shown that dog owners tend to be happier and healthier because the daily walks they give their dogs have health benefits for them, too.

However, owning a dog comes with responsibilities. Dogs need feeding, exercising, love and affection and someone to look after them when their owners go on holiday. One of the biggest complaints against dog ownership is dog-fouling. Despite fines of up to £1,000, there are still some irresponsible owners who do not clean up after their pets.

Dogs make good pets and they bring great rewards for many people, but they bring responsibilities too which should not be forgotten. Dogs are not like toys given at Christmas that can be thrown away when we tire of them — a dog is for life.

Get it?

The first paragraph outlines arguments 'for'. The second paragraph outlines arguments 'against'. The final paragraph gives a conclusion.

Write a similar balanced argument: Do cats make good pets?* Use a separate piece of paper for this.

*Or any other animal you choose.

A recount

When you've finished, give yourself a reward sticker!

Read the following recount:

When I arrived home at 7pm, I immediately knew something was wrong. The first thing I noticed was the light through the upstairs window which I knew I hadn't left on. Then I saw that the front door was wide open! I stepped nervously into the hallway and everything looked okay. Next, I went into the living room and to my dismay I saw that some burglars had broken in! Then I called the police.

Now answer these questions in complete sentences:

1. What time connectives have been used in the text? List them below.
   _____

2. What tense (past, present or future) is the text written in? Examine the verbs to find out.
   _____

3. Is the text written in the first, second or third person? Explain your answer.
   _____

Write a recount of a past event or experience that you can remember.
Use extra paper if needed.
   _____
   _____
   _____
   _____
   _____

Answers on page 32

Writing formal letters

When you've finished, give yourself a reward sticker!

Formal letter-writing follows a specific format:

WRITE YOUR ADDRESS HERE

THE RECIPIENT'S ADDRESS IS WRITTEN HERE

The Manager
Pizza Palace
Garlic Street
Doughton
ET7 UP1

WRITE THE DATE HERE

WRITE A FORMAL LETTER TO COMPLAIN ABOUT THE LACK OF TOPPINGS ON A PIZZA YOU BOUGHT FROM A FAST FOOD RESTAURANT. MAKE IT CLEAR WHY YOU ARE WRITING THIS LETTER. FOR EXAMPLE, DO YOU WANT A REFUND?

To Whom It May Concern,

_____

_____

_____

_____

_____

Yours faithfully,

_____

WRITE YOUR SIGNATURE HERE

Get it?

If you know the name of the person you are addressing, you end with 'Yours sincerely'.

STICK A REWARD STICKER HERE

Answers

Page 2. Know your nouns
1. I hurt my knee.
2. The paint is still wet.
3. Don't touch the exhibits!
4. Red is my favourite colour.
5. Can I have a biscuit?
6. Let's go for a walk.

There are several possible answers for this activity but your answers could include:
1. Look at that beautiful cherry tree in the garden.
2. She dressed up as her favourite character from the book.
3. I like those puppies in the basket.
4. The pencil case belongs to Ben. It's over there.
5. Catch the next train on platform 5.

Page 4. Adding adjectives
1. The clever detective caught the notorious thief.
2. Spectacular fireworks lit up the night sky.
3. A gigantic, hairy spider sat beside the nervous boy.
4. The excitable dog chased the terrified cat.
5. We had a delicious meal in a Japanese restaurant.
6. She wore a flowing dress and comfortable shoes.

Page 5. Perfect your pronouns
1. The reds beat the blues. They won by two points.
2. Jack loved the film when he saw it.
3. Bella is in my class. Do you know her?
4. Our neighbours are friendly when you get to know them.

1. The ice cream belongs to Harpreet. It's hers.
2. The snake belongs to us. It's ours.
3. The hat belongs to you. It's yours.
4. The car belongs to them. It's theirs.
5. The pencil case belongs to Ben. It's his.
6. The dog belongs to us. It's ours.
7. The book belongs to you. It's yours.
8. The ball belongs to me. It's mine.

Page 6-7. Verbs and adverbs
1. The racecar screeched around the track.
2. The mouse scampered under the sofa.
3. The waves crashed onto the rocks.
4. The girl whispered the secret to her friend.
5. The boy crept through the spooky house.

Here are some possible answers:
1. He looked fiercely at his opponent.
2. They spoke quietly on the phone.
3. She sang softly into the microphone.
4. The wind blew gently.
5. The volcano erupted violently.

Page 8. Adverbial phrases
Yesterday, at 11:58pm, a burglar broke into a jewellery shop on John Street.
It is claimed that the criminal threw a large rock through the front window and robbed the shop within minutes.

The jeweller, who lived above the shop, awoke to the sound of the shop alarm going off below his flat. By the time he ran downstairs, the burglar had escaped down the street, carrying a large bag of expensive digital watches.

The suspect has not yet been found.

Page 9. Playing with words
1. Someone who is always smiling = A ray of sunshine
2. Someone who is sneaky = A snake in the grass
3. Someone who stays up late = A night owl

Page 12-13. How to use apostrophes
1. the teacher's desk
2. Mum's purse
3. the artist's studio
4. the cat's whiskers

1. the girls' dog
2. the family's car
3. the players' changing room
4. the people's jobs
5. the babies' toys

1. We can't go yet.
2. She would've liked the taste.
3. The dog doesn't bite.
4. The car should've started.
5. It's not fair! / It isn't fair!

Page 14-15. Speech

"I think Dig is sick," said Tom. "He won't eat his dinner."
"Perhaps he's not hungry," replied Tom's mum.
"But he's *always* hungry!" said Tom. "And it's his favourite: marinated chicken chunks in juicy jelly."

The position of the exclamation marks can vary. Here is one possibility:

"Mum!" shouted Tom.
"Now what?" said Tom's mum.
"I know why Dig won't eat his dinner," said Tom.
"It's a new recipe. They've added vegetables! You know he hates vegetables!"

Answers

Page 16-17. Clauses and conjunctions
Here are some examples:
1. Dig didn't eat his dinner so Kit ate it instead.
2. Dig and Kit were friends but they were rivals, too.
3. Tom was worried when Dig hadn't eaten his food.
4. Mum wasn't paying attention because she was busy.

1. I put the dog on the lead <u>and</u> we went out for a walk.
2. It felt cold <u>although</u> it was sunny.
3. We played in the park <u>until</u> it was dark.
4. Mum was cross <u>when</u> I got home late.
5. I missed my programme <u>because</u> it came on earlier than usual.

1. I missed the last five minutes of the film. <u>Consequently</u>, I don't know how it ended!
2. I can come to your house. <u>However</u>, I can't stay for long.
3. Firstly, you mix the butter and the sugar. <u>Next</u>, you add the egg.
4. Dad did the shopping. <u>Meanwhile</u>, Mum was at work.
5. Do your homework now. <u>Later</u>, you can go swimming.

Page 18. Relative clauses
There are many possible answers. Here are some suggestions:
The friends<u>, who had known each other for 5 years,</u> decided to meet at the park.
The town<u>, where my dad lived,</u> was difficult to find.

Page 19. Parenthesis (using brackets, dashes and commas)
There are several possible answers. Here are some suggestions:
1. The staircase (735 steps) winds around the inside of the castle.
2. The Himalayas, where the largest mountain in the world is situated, are in Nepal.
3. The weather – thunder and lightning – spoiled our barbecue.
4. The car – annoyingly – would not start when we needed to get to school.

Page 20. Prefixes
1. aquarium, aquatic, aquamarine
2. vivisect, vivacious, vivid
3. geometry, geology, geography
4. biography, bionic, biological
5. octopus, octagon, octave
6. supermarket, supersonic, supervisor

Page 21. Suffixes
1. instructor
2. actor
3. conductor
4. hopeless
5. sleepless
6. restless
7. excitement
8. movement
9. agreement
10. immediately
11. suddenly
12. extremely

1. spiced
2. caring
3. later
4. biggest
5. swimming
6. stopped

Page 22. Different kinds of writing

Somehow <u>I</u> knew that today was going to be special, even though it started off like every other day – <u>I</u> was going to be late for school again!

To make chocolate brownies <u>you</u> need: flour, cocoa powder, eggs, butter and milk. But first, <u>you</u> need to find an adult to help <u>you</u>!

"I'm so happy!" <u>she</u> said. "I want to thank everyone who voted for me!" <u>They</u> cheered enthusiastically as <u>she</u> lifted the winner's trophy.

Page 26-27. Writing non-fiction
There are many possible answers. Here are some suggestions:
1. The cheetah is fast because it has long legs and an athletic body.
2. The cheetah is faster than the average car.
3. The wildebeest can outrun the cheetah because it can maintain its speed over longer distances.
4. Domestic cats no longer need to chase their dinner.
5. The text is written in present tense.

Page 29. A Recount
1. The following time connectives are used: 'when', 'immediately', 'first', 'then' and 'next' (the box below shows the connectives underlined).

<u>When</u> I arrived home at 7pm, I <u>immediately</u> knew something was wrong. The <u>first</u> thing I noticed was the light through the upstairs window when I knew I hadn't left it on. <u>Then</u> I saw that the front door was wide open! I stepped nervously into the hallway and everything looked okay. <u>Next</u>, I went into the living room and to my dismay I saw that some burglars had broken in! <u>Then</u> I called the police.

2. The text is written in the past tense.
3. The text is written in the first person because the pronouns 'I' and 'my' are used.